6/05

D1048646

Acting That
Matters

Acting That Matters

Barry Pineo

ALLWORTH PRESS
NEW YORK

© 2004 Barry Pineo

All rights reserved. Copyright under Berne Copyright Convention,
Universal Copyright Convention, and Pan-American Copyright
Convention. No part of this book may be reproduced, stored in a
retrieval system, or transmitted in any form, or by any means,
electronic, mechanical, photocopying, recording, or otherwise,
without prior permission of the publisher.

08 07 06 05 04   5 4 3 2 1

Published by Allworth Press
An imprint of Allworth Communications, Inc.
10 East 23rd Street, New York, NY 10010

Cover design by Derek Bacchus
Page composition by Sharp Designs, Lansing, MI
Typography by Integra

LIBRARY OF CONGRESS CATALOGING-IN-PUBLICATION DATA

Pineo, Barry.
   Acting that matters/ by Barry Pineo.
      ISBN: 1-58115-381-3
      p. cm.
   Includes index.

PN2061.P575 2004
792.02'8–dc22
                              2004012591

Printed in Canada

For James and Jesse

St. Louis Community College
at Meramec
LIBRARY

We must be the change we wish to see.

—*Mahatma Gandhi*

Do I contradict myself?
Very well, then, I contradict myself.
(I am large—I contain multitudes.)

—*Walt Whitman, "Song of Myself"*

Contents

A Note Before You Begin

FOR THOSE OF YOU WHO OBTAINED THIS BOOK because you want to learn how to act: You won't learn how to act by reading this book. You also won't learn how to act by taking a class or by getting a degree in acting—in other words, by taking multiple classes. While individuals attending institutions of higher education may graduate as more effective actors than when they first enrolled, most of the noticeable improvements in their acting effectiveness will come through having had the opportunity to act, not through much of anything their instructors may have provided.

So why should you buy this book? Because it can help you learn to act, more than any other book in existence. (Did you expect me to say something else?) And sure, classes can help you learn how to act, especially my workshop—if for no other reason than you'll get the opportunity to act. However, in the end, books and workshops and classes aren't the thing itself—the thing you seek—the ability to act effectively. Notice I didn't say, "the ability to be a great actor." I know great acting when I see it, but great acting is a function of time, place, script, director, fellow actors—a host of disparate elements coming together almost serendipitously. However, acting effectively isn't a function of coincidence. Acting effectively is a result of experience in and knowledge of the craft.

You want to learn to act? Then *act*. Go out and find a process and *act*. You say you can't get cast? Then you're not trying hard enough or you're not in the right place. If you're in Alaska, the opportunities to act are going to be few and far between. If you want to act, then go to a place where there are a lot of opportunities to act, like New York, Chicago, Seattle, Los Angeles, or even Austin, Texas. Still can't get cast? Then you're either totally lacking in talent, skill, or mental capacity, or you're not trying hard enough. Audition for everything, whether you're "right for it" or not. *Everything.* Still can't find a process? Then cast yourself. Write your own, produce your own, or write and produce and direct your own. Finding opportunities to act is easy, as long as you're not concerned with quality or cash, and if you want to learn how to act, then the quality of the production or the monetary compensation should be one of the last of your concerns. "Production values" are the most overrated thing about live theater. If we effectively tell stories with little else but live actors in front of a paying audience, production values won't even enter into the equation.

I recently read a story about a young man who asked an old guitarist to teach him how to play. The old guitarist told the young man that he could teach him everything he knew about playing guitar in fifteen minutes. Then, all the young man had to do was go home and practice for fifteen years.

That's the way I feel about acting. Reading this book will take you longer than fifteen minutes, but the sum of the knowledge contained herein can be communicated in about that much time. It can all be summed up in a few pages, which I do toward the end of the book. So, all you have to do is memorize those few pages, and then go practice for fifteen years.

You want to learn to act? Then *act*, and like anything else you care about in life, do it religiously and with intense dedication.

It really is that simple.

Introduction

AT THE VERY LEAST, most acting I see is little more than ego-centered self-indulgence. Blaming the actors for this state of affairs is a tempting proposition since, after all, they are the carriers of the play—the conduits, if you will—of the live theater experience. In an ultimate sense, it's in their hands. But I don't want to blame the actors, because I've been exposed on an intimate level to the way American acting is taught. More importantly, I've been exposed, on the most intimate level possible, to the culture in which the modern approach to acting is nurtured.

Recently, I had an actor with very limited experience join my workshop. I think it safe to say that he possessed little to no practical theater experience. He had done a little acting in high school, but that was many years before. For whatever reason, he felt compelled to act.

As a kind of initiation, any actor joining the workshop must come to the first session prepared to perform a number of one-minute monologues. This actor came to the workshop with three monologues, but only one of them was committed to memory, and that one not very well. On his first day, he got up and fumbled around a bit with an introduction—which really was no introduction at all—stumbled through the monologue he could recite, and then said he hadn't memorized the other two. After speaking with him about the importance of committing the text to memory, I gave him a task: The next weekend, he was to come to the workshop with all three monologues memorized; he would be able to introduce himself and his monologues, each with the title of the play, the playwright's name, and the name of the character he would be playing. I told him that, for each monologue, all he needed to do was look at a single focal point downstage and deliver the lines to that single focal point.

I called him the day before the next workshop session and gave him some encouragement. I told him to work, to work *hard*. I told him that, for whatever reason—the reason doesn't really matter— he was compelled to act, compelled to express himself in the most public, yet most intimate way possible. I told him that if he didn't give it his best shot, then got to the end of the workshop and decided that acting wasn't for him, he'd walk away never knowing if he actually could do it. But if he did the work, worked hard, worked as hard as he could, and then got to the end of the workshop and decided that acting wasn't for him, he could at least walk away knowing that he had done the best he could.

The next session, he volunteered fairly early on to present his monologues. He told us his name, the name of the first monologue, the playwright's name, and the name of the character he was presenting, then sat down, looked at the downstage focal point, and began to deliver the lines. After he got a couple of lines out, the rest of the workshop members laughed uproariously, and he lost his place, stopped, and apologized. After speaking with him about holding onto his concentration and not letting anything that we were doing as audience members interfere with his delivery of the text, he started again and managed, quite bravely and effectively, to get through the whole monologue— with the workshop members laughing, often with great gusto, throughout.

For me, it was a testament to the power of simply delivering the text. If the text works, quite often all an actor needs to do is deliver it loudly and clearly, without embellishment. If an actor trusts the text, quite often that's all he'll feel compelled to do. This particular actor was lucky in that he chose to start with a piece that worked quite well all on its own, with little help from him.

It was also a testament to the raw power of acting. If you're psychologically within the range of normal—and that's a very wide range—you can act. Anyone can. Acting is not about talent, although talent helps. Acting is not about skill, although skill helps. Acting is not about being a physically attractive specimen, although being a physically attractive specimen certainly helps.

Acting, more than anything else, is about sharing yourself with others. Theater is about storytelling, but acting is about allowing others to see who you are, really, with the masks you wear each day cast aside. Acting is about making connections—with yourself and with the other actors, and by extension, with the audience that comes to see the story you tell. Acting is about allowing something to simply be.

We're not interested in that in our culture. Western culture is not about life, not about allowing something to simply be. It's about death. It's about turning the living into the dead. It's not about diversity and our desire for it, however much we may preach about our liberality and our open arms. It's about competition. It's about us against them and me against you. In our culture, when you act, rather than being a person, you are a character. You don't have to worry about being yourself because you're not yourself—you're someone else. You don't have to concern yourself with that other actor onstage because that other actor is your competition. Not your partner, not your fellow, not your peer. Your competition. Your competition for the attention of the audience. Your competition for the positive review. Your competition for the yearly award. That's not a person—that's a competitor. That's not an animal, that's meat. That's not a tree, that's lumber. That's not a mountain, that's cans. We objectify everything we see. Not subjects, not living things that interact, but objects for us to consume and destroy.

This is not the truth. This is a system of living, not living itself. This is how we all have agreed to live. This is what we all participate in each day, knowingly or unknowingly. We have no choice. We have no freedom—or, at the very least, our freedom is an illusion. We can't choose to live outside the system. Well, we can, but we'll live homeless, or in a shack in Montana, sending bombs in the mail.

Participate in the system or die. That's our culture. It's that simple, it's that ugly, and it's not the truth. Things don't have to be this way. There is another way to live.

There's also another way to act.

The actor I've been writing about didn't really manage to get through his other two monologues. He got most of them out, but he stumbled and fumbled. For the next weekend, I asked him to really perform the tasks I'd assigned to him the previous weekend, with introductions, single focal points, and clean delivery of the texts. For the next three hours or so, he watched his fellow students present their monologues and scenes. Each of the others had moved on to scoring—marking their texts for beats, key phrases and words, and actions—and presenting their scores, a process a bit more complicated than just looking at a point and delivering memorized lines. He didn't say much. When the session was over, he came up to me and told me that he was ready. He wanted to score. He wanted to begin practicing the craft of acting. I think he felt this way because, earlier on, when he simply delivered that first monologue and got such a tremendous response, he saw that he could have an effect. On some level, he saw that connection is possible. Real connection, without all the dishonest, plastic, unnecessary embellishment you find in most acting. Quite suddenly, he perceived that he was not alone.

We're not alone. We're part of something that presents a façade of separateness and disconnection, when actually everything we see is connected to everything else in the most intimate way possible. Our seeming separation from each other and from everything around us is an illusion. Chaos—sure, there's chaos. Look at the history of the planet and you can see chaos, the element of chance, the Fates, if you will. Look at the moon— that's the clearest example. Now, look beyond it. What you see is, without question, the result of some awesome, eternal force organizing the seemingly random into a powerful order.

Acting is, as Stanislavsky said, work on one's self. Acting is becoming intimate with one's self. Acting is, to paraphrase that famous Greek maxim—knowing yourself. How can you pretend to know others unless you know yourself? How can you hope to help others see their interconnectedness if you're not connected to yourself? How can you hope to connect to other actors if you're constantly trying to be something other than what you are? Most theater I see is not a welcoming, an embrace, an interaction. Most theater I see is not even a giving. It's a taking. It's a "look at me." It's a "pay attention." It's not storytelling. It's not ritual. It's not communion.

It should be. If the theater we aspire to is a theater of connection, of communion, of ritual in its truest sense (and what a theater that is to aspire to, what a theater to strive for—a theater that is, in the best sense imaginable, magic), how can we give of ourselves without understanding what it is we are giving?

This book is about what we are giving. And the giving of it.

PART 1

Analysis

CHAPTER 1

Why We Are Who We Are

WE'RE ALL BORN STORYTELLERS. From the time we first learn to talk, we're telling stories, to ourselves and to others. I can't tell you how many stories my three-year-old has already told, mostly to himself, as he plays. I can't tell you how many times I've sat and listened to his stories. I can't understand the words, but I know he's telling stories. When someone is telling a story, you know he is even if you can't understand the words.

If we're all born storytellers, why is it that so many of us have such incredible difficulty acting? What is it that's holding us back? If we're all born to tell stories, and if theatrical acting is a form of storytelling, why is it seemingly so difficult to do it effectively?

I believe it isn't difficult, once you understand the tools and are used to manipulating them. It's that "getting used to the tools" that's so challenging, because the tools are us. An actor's instrument is *the self*. Unlike the carpenter or the painter or the musician, the actor possesses all of his tools within his body, and all actors, by the time they begin acting, have had those tools affected in so many different ways that it cannot be quantified. This is what leads to ineffective acting habits—our experiences. This is what makes acting so very, very difficult for so many, many people—our experiences.

From the moment you are pushed from the womb, and nowadays even before, you are being judged. "What a pretty baby!" "He's so nice and quiet!" "He's such a good boy!" One of my earliest childhood memories is my first stepfather yelling, "Can't you get that kid to shut up!" (Thus my inherent and well-developed ability to run off at the mouth.) I write this not in a search for sympathy, but only to point out that all of us to a certain extent, and some of us to a great extent, are products of our experiences. From the time we are very small, we look to others for affirmation, in order to learn how to behave, and we behave accordingly. Our instruments are molded *against our wills*. And not by people who have been prepared to train us or who care about or love us or are, at the very least, looking out for our best interests, but by *whoever happens to be there*. Often, it seems, by people who don't really care about us at all as living, breathing, feeling, human entities. By the time we get to acting, whether early or late in life, we have so much behind us and inside us that we often don't know ourselves. Most of us are so afraid, we don't even *want* to know ourselves. What might be there is too awful to contemplate.

I believe that's the primary reason that people are drawn to acting: When they were children, at one point or another, some essential intimacy was denied them.

Actors, deep down, want to know themselves. They are *compelled* to know themselves. To become intimate with themselves— and by extension, to become intimate with others. As many others as possible. But it all begins with the self. Acting is work on one's self.

Reaching Our Potential

How difficult to just let something *be*. How difficult to just leave something *alone*. Cultures exist in which children's basic needs are attended to—and then they're left to their own devices. Not judged or coerced or impelled or forced. Simply *let be*. And these cultures are perfectly fine, perfectly functioning (until, of course, the all-pervasive Western cultural system finds them out and gives them the choice to convert or die). And the children within these cultures grow and learn and become adults and have children—whom they simply *let be*.

We judge each other all the time. We constantly use words like "good" and "bad" and "right" and "wrong," and we use them unflinchingly and without thought to their actual connotations. In reality they mean almost nothing at all; they are nothing more than judgments of personal taste: "You have meaning for me" and "You don't have meaning for me," and in only the tersest, most common terms.

These kinds of value judgments serve little purpose. Any human being should use them only rarely, and only when surety is absolute. We should not judge each other in these terms because we can never truly know how violated any individual's experience has been. We should honor each other's efforts, period. And as for human beings in general: They're all worthy of our attention, from what we may consider the most corrupt to the most pristine. Never, ever judge a character you're tasked to present. Never, ever, except in the most extreme cases, judge another human entity as being unworthy of your attention, as being unworthy of life. Leave such judgments to the farce of the courts and the insidious texts of the fundamentalists.

Inside you, right now, there is unlimited potential that has been squashed. Inside each of us, right now, there is unlimited potential that has been shaped and molded and bound and tied and corrupted and flattered and ignored and used and discarded. We all, each of us, contain all the possibilities. Everything. Right here. Right now.

How to reach it? How to reach that potential?

That's what this technique really is all about. It's about accessing truth. It's about allowing the truth to live, in you and through you, the truth of life—and not just of your own life or of human life, but of the pattern of life itself.

We define ourselves by the stories that we tell. Once upon a time, our stories were about a family of gods, and life was patterned after the behavior of those gods. Once, the earth was the center of the universe, and life was patterned with that in mind. Now, one of our stories is evolution and another is the Big Bang. The stories we tell define us, make us who we are, and as life follows a pattern, so stories follow a pattern. *Storytelling* follows a pattern—the pattern of life.

The theater and life should be the same, should work the same way, because the theater *is* life. Storytelling *is* life. If we wish to tell stories effectively, we must recognize the patterns of life and act on them, because when we do, we become a reflection of eternal truth, the eternal truth of life, and eternal truth is what storytelling is all about. Theatrical storytelling is an ultimately spiritual act, and acting is, or should be, the highest of callings.

An Answer to a Question

Found herein is an answer to the question, What is acting? Understand that it's just "an" answer—not "the" answer. Anyone that tells you they have "the" answer to this particular question is looking for a cult member, not an actor. Acting teachers, it seems, often are looking for acolytes rather than actors. They want to make actors dependent on them rather than independent of them. They want to make actors believe an authority of some kind must stamp "APPROVED" on their acting. Nothing could be further from the truth. While an authority may help you begin your journey, you don't need an authority, because the journey you take is ultimately yours and yours alone. What you really need is not an authority but an understandable, immediately applicable, wide-ranging technique, and that's exactly what you'll find here: a fully formed, self-contained, easily grasped process for approaching text and presenting it in an effective manner. For that's what acting is at its most essential: presenting text in an effective manner. Any text. *Every* text. When you see a great performance, or a good one, or simply an adequate one, in the theater or on film or wherever, more often than not, you're seeing text presented in an effective manner. When I say effective acting, I'm simply talking about acting that works. And if a piece of acting works, it's working in a way very much the same as any other acting that works—according to a pattern. According to a set of understandable, albeit flexible, rules.

I'm writing about a technique, so I'm going to get *technical*. That means there are sections of this book that are going to be difficult, at first glance, to wade through. Take a look at the outline in appendix A. (I'm serious. Whenever I suggest you look at something, take a look. Whenever I suggest you try something, try it. If I didn't want you to look at or try what I was suggesting,

I wouldn't have taken the time to ask you to do so. So, take a look at the outline in appendix A...Right *now*.)

That's it. That's the technique. People have told me that it's formulaic and that, because of its formulaity, it cannot have the quality that all effective acting has: spontaneity. As for formulaity—well, of course it's formulaic. Storytelling *is* formulaic. Writing *is* formulaic. Because acting is, in a sense, the vocal delivery of writing—the presentation of text, if you will—it follows that the acting process will contain formulaic elements. And as for spontaneity—take a look at the outline of "Activation" in appendix A. Spontaneity—actual, real, in-the-flesh spontaneity—is exactly what I seek.

After taking a good look at appendix A, you may think that the technique is difficult, but it isn't. It may not look easy, but once you understand it, it *is* easy, and it *works*. It allows you a clean, simple way into any character because it never asks you to be anything but what you are.

It is work, though. Hard, sometimes arduous work. Because in order to act effectively, you must overcome the ineffective habits you've built up over a lifetime of corruption. You do this by using a part of your instrument that is of paramount importance and that more than a few actors simply aren't using to its full potential: your mind. And when you're done with the book and you fully understand the technique (well, not just understand it, but know it, in your bones, in your blood, in your soul), you will act effectively. First time, every time. And I'm not talking about "acting well" or "acting brilliantly" or "being an artist"—that's all so subjective and ultimately meaningless. I'm talking about simply presenting text effectively. That's the work. In a sense, that's all acting is.

But it isn't, as well. It's so much more. It's about overcoming the life of your past, which is corrupt almost beyond comprehension. It's about learning to accept and love yourself for who you are. The key word there is "accept." With all your flaws, which often are what make you interesting, and with all your assets, which often are what make you interesting.

Accept yourself. Love yourself for who you are. You are unique. No one else like you exists and, once you are gone from this place, will ever exist again. You are valuable just being who you are. You cannot, in fact, be anyone else.

If you came to acting to hide, you came to the wrong place. Think about it logically. It's you up there, all on your own, all by yourself. There's no place to hide. And you don't have to.

You shouldn't even want to.

Just be who you are.

And if people don't like you, well, to *hell* with them. People are what messed you up in the first place.

CHAPTER 2

Craft and Technique

OFTEN, IT SEEMS, logic is abandoned when it comes to the craft of acting. The idea that eternal truths exist also doesn't seem to be much in fashion among people with a theatrical bent. At least in America, it seems, truth has become relative and situational. While I'm a great believer in relativity as it concerns certain subjects, and a sometime advocate of situational morality, I also believe, completely, wholeheartedly, and with great certainty, that eternal truths exist, and that they certainly exist when it comes to theatrical storytelling and the craft of acting. This book, as much as anything else, is an attempt to bring logic to what has become an illogical undertaking.

> **craft** I : ART, SKILL; also, an occupation requiring special skill.
> **technique** I : the manner in which technical details are treated or special physical movements are used.
> **technical** [Gk *technikos* of art, skillful, fr. *techne* art, craft skill] I : having special knowledge.

These were taken from a very old dictionary—twenty-six years old, to be exact. It's quite possible the definitions have changed significantly, but I doubt it.

Some observations: "Art" is a part of the definition of "craft," along with "skill." Craft requires "special skill." "Technique" shares a root with "technical," the definition of which also contains art, craft, and skill. Craft requires "special skill." Technique requires "special knowledge." I detect a pattern here. Art, craft, and technique seem to be married to each other, to be interdependent.

Given the definitions above, if you are the element at the center of a live art form, can you agree that you need special skills in order to contribute in a meaningful way to that art form? (And I'm not trying to be a sarcastic here, but I don't see the words "instinct" or "talent" anywhere up there, especially in those definitions.)

You need an actor to make theater. What else do you need? An audience, yes? What else? The actor, the audience—the audience watches the actor, while the actor—*does something*. Is that enough? If there's just an actor up there doing something, is that enough? How about if the actor is doing something with a purpose? Is that enough? It's an improvement, sure, but ultimately, in order for theater to be the art form we recognize as theater, an audience watching an actor doing something with a purpose is not enough. The audience needs some kind of *story*. The audience has come to the theater with exactly that expectation—to see a story. Going further, the vast majority of the time, the audience that comes to see live theater comes with the expectation not just of *seeing* a story, but of *hearing* a story, for words are at the heart of most every piece of live theater in existence. Almost all live theater deals with text of some kind. Almost all live theater deals with a lot of text almost all of the time.

So, you're the element at the center of the art form known as theater, and you have to deal with a lot of text almost all of the time. What special skills—what *technique*—do you, as an actor, need in order to contribute in a meaningful way to the art?

You need to deliver a lot of text—a lot of *words*—and it follows that you need to be able to speak loudly and clearly enough so that everyone can hear and understand what you're saying. Since theater deals with a lot of text, audiences come to the theater expecting to *hear* a lot of text. If the audience can't hear the text it came for, its expectations will be dashed and it most likely will have great difficulty enjoying the play. If it can hear the text but can't understand it, then you're in the same quickly-sinking-and-soon-to-be-riding-the-bottom-of-the-river boat.

So, if you accept that theater is an art, acting is a craft, that in order to be successful as an actor, you require a technique, and finally, that your first job as an actor is to deliver text, it makes sense that, next to one's mind, the first and likely most important tool that a theater actor can possess is a loud, clear voice. Note that I did not say a *film* actor. A film actor requires neither a loud nor a particularly clear voice. As practically anyone with even the slightest experience in film acting will tell you, theatrical acting is the more difficult of the two. If you can master acting in the theater, acting in film will seem like a stroll in the finest of forests.

CHAPTER 3

The Parts
of a Story

In a sense, this statement is a fallacy: Actors are special people. Actors are no more special than anyone else. Most have no special skills, although many would like us to think that they do. Many want us to believe that, in some sense, they are better connected to and freer with their emotions than other people, but that isn't true either. I know more than a few actors, some who make their living acting, who have no more conscious technique or skill than anyone within the range of normal you'd meet walking on the street on any given day. Experience, certainly. Conscious technique and/or skill, no.

Why, then, are they actors? Because they *chose* to be, that's all. They might have chosen that path because they looked in a mirror and thought, " I'm attractive. I can act." They might have chosen acting because someone told them they had a "talent" for it, or they believed they had it. They might have chosen acting, as many do, because they were denied attention at some crucial point in their maturation, and acting is arguably a way to get attention. A lot of attention.

Certainly, talented actors exist. In other words, people exist who have an aptitude for acting. But the fact that you have an aptitude for something doesn't necessarily mean that you have technique, only that you have natural skill. Technique involves having special knowledge, and knowledge and talent are not the same thing. If you can acquire the special knowledge inherent in any craft, then you can become an effective practitioner of that craft.

Next to the mind, the first tool of the actor is a loud, clear voice. If you already have a loud, clear voice, then you have a talent. If you don't have a loud, clear voice, then you don't have this particular talent. If you desire a loud, clear voice, can you obtain one? Certainly. It may take some work, but all of this acting stuff, like any craft, takes some work.

A theatrical actor needs a loud, clear voice because being able to communicate text effectively is central to what an actor in the theater does. The play's the thing. Plays are stories, stories are made from words, and an actor in the theater tells stories by vocally delivering the words in the texts of plays. Isn't that what an actor in the theater is being asked to do almost all of the time?

The Commonality of Story Structure

Is there anything that can be said about story that we all can agree on? Surely this, at least: Most stories—I would even venture to say the vast majority, if not 100 percent—have a beginning, a middle, and an end.

In other words, stories have parts. Beginning, middle, end—parts. All stories can be broken down into parts. Can we substitute the word "analyzed" for "broken down into parts?" Would that be fair?

From the old dictionary:

> **analyze** 1a : to ascertain the components of or separate into component parts.

All stories can be analyzed because all stories can be broken down into parts.

What are the parts of a story in the theater? We have plays. Plays have acts. Acts have scenes. Scenes have sentences. Sentences have words. Words in sentences are connected to and separated from each other by punctuation. These, at base, are the parts of a play.

Those of you who have taken an English class (and my bet is that is most anyone who happens to be reading this) are probably familiar with the common outline of the structure of a story, which often looks like this: exposition, building action, climax, denouement.

The exposition of a story is the basic information that a listener needs in order to understand the story. At some point during any exposition, a problem or set of problems is introduced that will be addressed during the course of the story. The introduction of the problem, or set of problems, is commonly referred to as the "inciting incident." Usually, the problem or set of problems consists of two people (or two groups of people) wanting two different and opposing things. Because the opposing forces want different things, "dramatic tension" is introduced into the story. Exposition is the most important part of almost any story, for without the exposition, understanding most stories is difficult, if not impossible.

The building action of a story involves the addressing of the central problem by the two opposing forces, and during this part of a story, dramatic tension increases. The climax arrives when the central problem is addressed in some manner that often involves resolution of some kind. Almost always the briefest portion of a play, the denouement, or falling action, shows the aftermath of the resolution.

Macrocosm / Microcosm

In the theater, and in almost any other art form involving storytelling, you will find these four common story elements, and what occurs in the macrocosm is reflected in the microcosm. An act of a play will almost always have these same four elements, as will a scene. Some passages of dialogue will have these same four elements, and in almost every instance, the most important part will be the exposition, the "plot," the necessary information the audience must possess in order to understand the playing out of the central problem.

Sounds simple, doesn't it? It is. Exposition, building action, climax, denouement. But still, after all this "analysis," we have not arrived at, or ferreted out, one further part of a play that indicates yet another breaking down of a story into parts. For an actor, it is a tool secondary in importance only to a mind within the range of normal and a loud, clear voice. In the theater, this essential part of a story is commonly referred to as a "beat."

CHAPTER 4

Beats

I HOPE THAT AT THIS POINT, you'll agree that plays are subject to analysis. But why should actors analyze them? Just because they're subject to analysis doesn't necessarily mean actors have to analyze them. It's conceivable that an actor can simply memorize the lines, go onstage, spit them out, and give a perfectly adequate performance. That seems to be the way more than a few actors approach their craft. But if that approach to acting were an effective one, why, then, does so much of the theater we see not work? If the theater is a vibrant, valuable, attractive proposition, why aren't people clamoring to get in the door to see live theatrical presentations? I'm guessing here, but could it be a lack of craft? A lack of knowledge and skill on the part of the participants?

If you have talent, why would you possibly need skill? Why would you possibly need knowledge? Why would you need to apply your knowledge and skill to a text and make a plan for how to present it, especially when you can simply rely on your native talent and go out and wing it?

Well, how about this: The playwright made a plan. The playwright made a detailed plan—the play. And if the play works—like *Antigone* works, like *Hamlet* works, like *Hedda Gabler*, *The Cherry Orchard*, *Death of a Salesman*, *Long Day's Journey into Night*, *The Glass Menagerie*, *American Buffalo*, *Buried Child* work—I believe it would behoove us to become as familiar with the plan of the playwright as it is possible to be. The most obvious way to do that is to *analyze* any given play, and your analysis should begin with the beat—the most basic, and most important, analytical tool an actor possesses.

A beat, like an act and a scene, is a part of a story, but a much smaller part than any of the latter. Keeping in mind that, almost without exception, the rules of acting are flexible and situational, usually a beat will have the same general structure as the story that surrounds it: a beginning (exposition), middle (building action), and end (climax, denouement). Not all beats will have this structure, but if you examine most individual beats, you will find exposition, building action, and climax. Some have a denouement—a release of tension from the climax—but it often comes only in a phrase at the end of a beat. Keep in mind that I'm talking *within a beat* here. *Within a beat*, you can find exposition, building action, climax, and occasionally denouement.

Next to a mind within the range of normal and a loud, clear voice, the ability to recognize a beat is the most important tool an actor can possess because the beats and the form that they take often dictate the use of the presentational tools outlined herein. For instance, along with language, the beats of a scene establish the rhythm and tempo of a scene. The beats dictate when the actor must be silent and physically still and when relatively larger physical movements may be utilized. The beats often dictate when volume needs to increase or decrease. In short, the beats have a tremendous, often overwhelming influence on the presentation of the text.

Examples of Beats in a Monologue

A monologue, if you will, is a little scene, a little story; like a scene (an act, a play), a monologue works according to the same formula. Writing is so formulaic that, if you examine a large number of monologues, you'll find that the majority of them that last around one minute have four beats. Look at the monologue from Shakespeare's *Macbeth* in appendix B. The slash marks ("/") indicate where the beats begin and end. (Keep in mind that the first beat always begins at the beginning of a piece and the last beat always ends at the end of a piece, so there is no need to mark the beginning of the first beat and the end of the last beat.) For now, ignore the bolding and underlining in the monologue and pay attention strictly to the beats.

The first beat of the monologue consists of a single sentence:

> To be thus is nothing,
> But to be safely thus.

While it may seem somewhat confusing to begin here, occasionally you will mark only a single sentence as a beat. (Note that the final beat of the *Macbeth* monologue also consists of only a single sentence.) This is the exception to the rule, however, and the three beats in the middle of this particular monologue cleave strictly to the idea of a beat having an exposition, building action, climax, and denouement.

Look at the second beat:

> Our fears in Banquo stick deep,
> And in his royalty of nature reigns that
> Which would be fear'd. 'Tis much he dares,
> And to that dauntless temper of his mind,
> He hath a wisdom that doth guide his valor
> To act in safety. There is none but he
> Whose being I do fear, and under him
> My genius is rebuk'd, as it is said
> Marc Antony's was by Caesar.

The first line in the beat is the exposition of the beat: "Our fears in Banquo stick deep." The rest of the beat is a development of that single idea. Note the repetition of the idea: "And in his royalty of nature reigns that which would be fear'd"; "There is none but he whose being I do fear." The beat is about Macbeth's fears concerning Banquo. It begins with that idea and develops the idea in the following two sentences. It climaxes with the phrase "my genius is rebuk'd," and this idea is built up to within the beat as Macbeth mentions Banquo's wisdom and the nature of its guidance.

If you examine the third beat of the monologue, you'll note the structural similarities to the second beat: the exposition ("he chid the sisters . . . and bade them speak to him"); the building action (the sisters speak to Banquo about his prospects, then to

Macbeth about his); and the climax ("no son of mine succeeding"). Should you take the time to examine the fourth beat, you will find exactly the same pattern.

Rules for Marking Beats

When attempting to mark beats in a script, look for the following:

1. *A complete line of thought*—the second beat in the Macbeth monologue is about Macbeth's fears of Banquo; the third beat is about what the witches said; the fourth beat is about the fate Macbeth has brought upon himself. A complete line of thought is *by far* the greatest indicator of a beat.

2. *Repetition of words, phrases, and/or ideas*—in the second beat of the Macbeth monologue, Macbeth uses the word "fear" in three different ways.

3. If you're having trouble finding the beats in a monologue or are in any way unsure of where to mark the beats, *instead of working forward, work backward*.

For any given script, there is only one set of beats. While it's certainly possible that one actor will score a given script for beats differently than another, and the two actors thus end up with different sets of beats, I still would assert that there is only one set of beats. One, or both, of those actors will have marked some of their beats incorrectly.

Scoring a Scene for Beats

Take a look at the scene score in appendix C. When scoring a scene, you score the beats for *both* characters (or *all* the characters, if there are more than two). Although most of the scene in appendix C has been scored for only a single character, note that the beats are scored for the *entire* scene, or for both characters. Take a look at what is marked as beat #4. The beat is about Goldie's sense of smell, but instead of one character, it involves two characters speaking a total of five lines, and all five of the lines center on a complete line of thought. Look at what is marked as beat #11. This beat is about how Marnie got interested in bugs, and again, it involves two characters speaking a total of four lines (counting the monologue as a "line"), all four of which center on a complete line of thought. As outlined above, that is, in fact, the most important indicator of a beat: a complete line of thought.

Analyzing a story and breaking it down into its component parts is commonly referred to as "scoring." The words "analysis" and "score" are, or should be, interchangeable for actors. While marking the beats is the most important step in scoring, the second step is almost equally important: marking the phrases.

CHAPTER 5

Key Phrases

EVERY WORD IN A TEXT HAS SOME IMPORTANCE; otherwise, the playwright wouldn't have included it. Outside of technical requirements (set pieces, props, costumes), in the words of a play the playwright provides everything you need to tell a story. However, only the most argumentative among us wouldn't agree that some words are more important than other words.

Generalizations Regarding the Text of a Play

Below, I've outlined some generalizations about the text of a play:

- The audience depends on the words of a play.
- If everything weighs the same, everything weighs nothing.
- All the lines in a play are important.
- Some lines are more important than other lines.
- All phrases are important.
- Some phrases are more important than other phrases.
- All words are important.
- Some words are more important than other words.

If every line were as important as every other line, if every phrase, every word, were as important as every other phrase and word, little variety would exist in any actor's vocal delivery, and all plays, when performed, would sound flat. The generalizations outlined above fall right in line with the four-part idea of story development, with the idea that some things in stories are more important than other things, and with the idea that it's possible to pick out—to *analyze*—what is and isn't most important in any given story. I would go so far as to say that it's of *paramount* importance that an actor is able to pick out what is and isn't important in any given story and, in turn, to know the most effective way to deliver that important information to an audience.

Think of it this way: After you've seen a play or a movie or read a novel and you wish to tell someone else about the experience, you don't recite the play or movie or novel to them verbatim; rather, you tell them the important parts of the plot (never giving away the ending, of course, unless what you saw wasn't worth seeing). In other words, it's possible to tell the entire story without repeating it word for word or event for event. Of course, the story you tell isn't the story you read or saw, but it is in the sense that you hit all the high points.

Choosing Key Phrases

In order to score a play for beats, you need *all* the lines, the same way you need to read or see the *entire* story if you're going to be able to tell someone else about it. But the next step in the scoring process is like the step you take when you tell a friend about what you read or saw: outlining the high points, which, in the case of a play, we'll refer to as "key phrases" and "key words."

Key phrases are exactly what they sound like—the most important phrases in your lines. In almost every instance, key phrases will contain plot information, "plot" being the lines concerning the story, the "exposition," the necessary information the audience needs to hear and understand in order to follow what the characters are doing. Key phrases can also contain information that's important only to your character and information that's important only to the theme (the set of ideas that the playwright utilizes in telling the story), but in any play, key phrases concerning character and theme are sparse. In almost every instance, a key phrase will contain strictly plot information, because the audience has come to the theater to see, and more importantly, hear a story, and lines that concern plot center on exactly that—the story.

Once a text is scored with beats, an actor knows where the smallest parts of the story begin and end. Since we know that the exposition—the *plot*—is the most important element in a story, and since we know that the exposition is going to come at or near the beginning of the story, it follows that most, if not all, of the important information in a beat is going to come at or near the beginning of a beat. This is because the microcosm—the *beat*—reflects the macrocosm—the *story*.

Look at the *Macbeth* monologue in appendix B and examine the second beat. The key phrases are bolded (when working with a script using pencil, however, you *circle* key phrases). Here are the key phrases:

> Our fears in Banquo stick deep
> 'Tis much he dares
> There is none but he
> Whose being I do fear

These three phrases tell the story, in miniature, of this beat of the monologue. Once you have marked the key phrases in any piece of text, whether for a single beat or for the entire text, you should be able to read only those phrases you have circled and get the story of that piece of text *in miniature*. Here are all the key phrases from the Macbeth monologue:

> To be thus is nothing
> But to be safely thus
> Our fears in Banquo stick deep
> 'Tis much he dares
> There is none but he
> Whose being I do fear
> He chid the sisters
> And bade them speak to him
> They hail'd him father to a line of kings
> Upon my head they plac'd a fruitless crown
> No son of mine succeeding. If 't be so

> For Banquo's issue have I 'fil'd my mind
> And mine eternal jewel
> the seeds of Banquo kings
> come, fate

Is the story there? It certainly is in the beginning and the middle, but it seems to peter away at the end, and for good reason. Shakespeare's language is often difficult for the modern ear to comprehend, and frequently in Shakespeare, no matter how much time you may take saying something and no matter how important it may or may not be to the story, the modern ear won't be able to translate it. In such instances, the most effective choice is to circle what *can* be understood and leave the rest uncircled. This is the case with much of the fourth beat of the *Macbeth* monologue. "Put rancors in the vessel of my peace" and "given to the common enemy of man" aren't phrases that a modern ear will immediately understand, so they aren't circled.

Take another look at the monologue and note how the bolded (circled) material groups itself *around the beat changes*. In every instance, something at or close to the beginning of each beat is bolded. In three instances, the last phrase of a beat is bolded. While there are three instances in which material in the middle of a beat is bolded, only one of them involves material that may not be significant in the plot ("and mine eternal jewel"), and this speaks directly to that list of generalizations outlined above. If everything weighs the same, everything weighs nothing. If you have a long section of a monologue where nothing seems of great importance, then in order to break up the tempo of the monologue, and thus add rhythm and variety to your vocal delivery, you need to pick out something that seems of *greatest* importance. In this instance, I chose the phrase "and mine eternal jewel," since it involves what is most important to Macbeth: his soul.

You'll find this to be true in almost every piece of text you encounter: You'll circle a key phrase at or near the beginning of a beat, since that's where the exposition will be found. While you may circle material in the middle and at the end of a beat, you won't do so with the same consistency as you will at the beginnings of beats. And again, this very neatly mirrors the idea of the most important information (the exposition, the plot) coming at the *beginning* of the beat (or scene, or play). The microcosm reflects the macrocosm. When confronted with a beat in which no plot information is present, you'll circle something at or near the beginning of the beat in order to add vocal variety to the beat and, more importantly, to provide, in presentation, an aural cue to the listener that a new part of the story is beginning—but I'm getting ahead of myself now.

Hopefully at this point you can see the importance of marking the beats correctly in any given play, for the beats will lead you straight to what's most important in the story. The converse is also true: If you can pick out the phrases that are most important, you'll be able to find where the beats change, because the key phrases will primarily group themselves around the beat changes.

Rules Regarding Key Phrases

Almost invariably, key phrases will comprise 35 to 40 percent of the words in any given script. I've found this to be true across the board, with little deviation, and particularly so with monologues, of which I've scored, or examined the scores, for hundreds. If you've effectively scored a text for key phrases, your score will contain these two elements:

- The key phrases will primarily group themselves at or close to the beat changes (almost invariably at or near the beginnings of beats, sometimes in the middle of beats, sometimes at the end).
- The key phrases will comprise 35 to 40 percent of the words in the script (not nearly as important as the way key phrases are *grouped*).

Pay close attention to that 35 to 40 percent of the words *in the script*. It may very well be that your particular character says nothing that's of great importance to the plot, and if this is the case, then nothing you say will be circled because nothing you say is important. There's an old saying in theater: There are no small parts, only small actors. It's a cute saying, but actually there *are* small parts. There are small actors, too. Don't be one of them. The theater isn't about you. It's about the story that you tell.

CHAPTER 6

Key Words

IF YOU ARE AN ACTOR, YOUR ART IS IN WORDS. Words comprise the most important commodity you deal in, to put it as forcefully and culturally as possible. If you wish to be an effective actor, you need to immerse yourself in words and their meanings.

The next part of your analysis is, in a sense, the tiniest part, and one that is most subject to deviation, but not inordinately so. Once you have circled all the key phrases, look for key words and underline them. Keep in mind that key words are *not* key phrases. Key phrases are two or more words that you circle. While you can have a key word *within* a key phrase, you can't have a key phrase within a key word because key words are single words that you stress when delivering text. Like key phrases, key words help the audience receive the story, but in a much quicker, more economical way than key phrases.

You will, on average, key one word out of every eight words, but if you participate in the craft of acting over an extended period of time, you'll be confronted with more than a few instances in which you may key every other word (or no words at all) in any given phrase. This will depend on the rhythm of the piece and the importance of any given phrase. Be careful, though. Keying every other word on a consistent basis will drive an audience up a wall. One out of eight, or a number falling within a digit either way of eight (i.e., one out of seven or one out of nine), is the general standard. This means that, in any given line of Shakespeare verse, you will key a word every eighth word, or approximately one per line of verse.

Choosing Key Words

When keying words, look for what I call "sense words." As an example, look at the first two lines of the Macbeth monologue:

> To be thus is nothing,
> But to be safely thus.

With the exception of the last phrase, this entire monologue is about Macbeth's fear of Banquo. He fears Banquo because Banquo, or Banquo's sons, could be a threat to his crown. Macbeth, in this line, and even in the monologue as a whole, is thinking of his own *safety*. I've already circled the entire line as a key phrase, which means that, through the effective utilization of the presentational tools, I am going to find a way to put this information across clearly to an audience. Assisting me in my attempt at clarity will be my keying of the word "safely." Ten words in the sentence, one key word—the *ninth* word (one out of nine).

One could argue that keying the first instance of "thus" or keying "nothing" also could put across the meaning, or perhaps keying all three words. But if everything weighs the same, everything weighs nothing. Standing on their own, which of these three words contributes most to the telling of the story for this particular passage? With little question, it is the word "safely." As for the first instance of "thus" and the word "nothing," these are what I will refer to as "secondary keys." You should not mark secondary keys because a score should be something that is fairly simple, and with work, easily recalled. Rather, you should be aware that they exist and allow them some vocal stress when you deliver the text. The most common way to key a word is to give it slightly more volume than the words that surround it. Primary keys, relatively speaking, receive more volume than the words that surround them; secondary keys receive less volume than primary keys, but still more than the words that surround them.

Read the line "To be thus is nothing, but to be safely thus" out loud, not stressing any one word over any other word. That is, give every word in the line the same amount of vocal stress. Delivered in this way, the line sounds "flat"; this makes sense because, in your delivery of it, everything weighed the same. Now try reading the line again, but this time, give more stress— more *volume*—to the word "safely." You will find that the line not only makes more sense to your ear, but the word "safely" stands out in importance. Try reading the line again, giving slightly more stress to the first instance of "thus" and to the word "nothing," and giving the most stress to the word "safely." Now the line seems filled with sense and, more importantly, with real thought and consideration. Now the line has *rhythm*.

If you are an actor, your art is in words.

When looking for key words, choose only those words that are by far the most important in any given text. You may find many single words that you believe are of utmost importance, but very few of them actually will be. Those words you come across that are of secondary importance are the words you will key in a secondary way to add rhythm, and thus texture, to your vocal delivery. Do not, however, mark secondary keys in your score. Only mark primary keys. Keep your score as uncluttered and simple as possible.

Take a look at the next few keys in the *Macbeth* monologue. "Fear" is keyed for an obvious reason: The whole monologue centers on Macbeth's fears and his safety from those fears. "Deep" is chosen because it accents the quality of Macbeth's fear. "Would" is chosen to accentuate Macbeth's definition of that quality in Banquo that is fearful. What are the secondary keys? My bet is that, if you read the line containing the keys "fear," "deep," and "would," you'll end up keying "reigns" in a secondary way. The rhythm established by choosing those three primary keys almost forces you to key "reigns" in a secondary manner.

Checking Your Key Words

Once you believe you have an effective set of key words, as with key phrases, look through the monologue, reading only the key words, and see if, like the phrases, they tell the story in miniature. Here are the key words from the *Macbeth* score: safely, fears, deep, would, wisdom, guide, safety, he, fear, rebuk'd, Caesar, chid, me, him, father, line, head, fruitless, barren, son, If't, fil'd,

murder'd, them, enemy, kings, fate, utterance. Certainly, much
of the sense of the monologue is contained in this set of words,
and where there are exceptions—would, he, me, him, If't—the
exceptions tend to modify or be directly connected with other
chosen sense words. As much as possible, you should avoid keying
pronouns like "he" and "I" and conjunctions like "if" and "and,"
for there is less "sense" in these words than in words like "fear"
and "rebuk'd" and "fruitless." Don't avoid pronouns and conjunctions altogether, but every time you choose to key a pronoun or a
conjunction, take a look at the other, more sense-filled words
around them to see if you've really made the most effective
choice possible.

Caesuras

Finally, do not mark two consecutive words as key words unless
they are separated by something that acts as a caesura. For our
purposes, a "caesura" is a punctuation mark or other indication in
the text that prompts a cessation of vocalization (i.e., a period,
semicolon, dash, etc., or something written parenthetically by the
playwright, such as "Pause," "Long Pause," "Silence," etc.). Trying
to key two words in a row without some kind of caesura falling
between the two words is extremely awkward—one or the other
almost always will demand more stress, and the one that demands
the stress will be the key. If you are tempted to underline two
words in a row, and those two words are not separated by
a caesura, then you have a key phrase, not a key word, and you
circle the phrase.

A Key Word Game

If you've been in the theater for a while, you've probably heard
actors playing the "key" game. While this is not an organized
sport, you'll sometimes find actors experimenting with keys in
order to make their peers laugh by making the lines sound funny
in an awkward way. For instance, using the line from the *Macbeth*
monologue, you'll find actors experimenting like this: "*To* be thus
is nothing *but* to be safely thus." In other words, they'll put the

keys in places where they obviously are not meant to fall. While often done just as a joke, this is actually a useful exercise. If you're ever confused about where a key word should fall, approach each word in the line or phrase individually, like this: *to* be thus is nothing; to *be* thus is nothing; to be *thus* is nothing; to be thus *is* nothing; to be thus is *nothing*. In other words, examine the possibilities thoroughly, then pick the one that makes the most sense, both to your ear and to the story.

If there is an art in the craft of acting, it is being able to discern what words are most important in any given text and then utilizing an effective method in presenting them. The tools outlined above—the beat, the key phrase, and the key word—are the most concrete analytical tools available to an actor to assist her in discerning what's most important in any given piece of text. However, there are two additional analytical tools that can go far in allowing actors to have confidence in their analytical choices. One is the ability to discern and articulate the story in any given beat.

CHAPTER 7

Story

I DON'T ASK ACTORS TO WRITE THE STORY ON THEIR SCORES. As much as possible, a score needs to be simple, and if you're marking the beats, the phrases, and the key words (and the actions—I'll get to them shortly), you're already putting more than enough information on the page. I do, however, believe that discerning and articulating the story of any given beat is an essential tool for an actor, for two reasons: (1) It allows the actor to confirm the choices he has made concerning the beats; and (2) It guides the actor in choosing the key phrases and key words in any given piece of text. You should be able to tell the story of any given beat using the following form: "This beat is about _____." Fill in the blank with eight words or less. If you're tempted to fill in the blank with more than eight words, you most likely haven't scored that particular beat in an effective manner. Also, when articulating the story in any given beat, as much as possible, use the language of the play to tell the story. Here is the story of the *Macbeth* monologue, written from Macbeth's point of view:

> *The first beat is about being safe as king.* (To be thus—to be king—is nothing, but to be *safe* as king is something. Again, as much as possible, use the language of the play to tell the story.)
> *The second beat is about my fear of Banquo.* (See the language of the play in there?)
> *The third beat is about what the witches said concerning Banquo and me.*
> *The fourth beat is about the fate I may have brought upon myself.*
> *The fifth beat is about making fate my champion.*

Let's look closely at a few of these. The first beat is about being safe as king. In fact, one could make the argument (I already have, but bear with me) that the entire monologue is about being safe as king, and that argument is a fruitful and instructive one: The "exposition"—being safe as king—comes at the beginning of the monologue. I have chosen to circle the entire beat ("To be thus is nothing, but to safely thus"), thus making it a key phrase. The beat is about being "safe" as "king," so I have chosen to key the words "safely" and "thus," "thus" being a reference to my present kingly state. This is an excellent example of how articulating the story of a beat can point you straight toward what is most important in a text.

The second beat is about my fear of Banquo. My key phrases focus strictly on this subject: "Our fears in Banquo stick deep" (the exposition of the beat); "'Tis much he dares"; "There is none but he whose being I do fear." The key words also center on the fear of Banquo articulated in the story and the reasons for that fear: fears, deep, would, wisdom, guide, safety, he, fear, rebuk'd, Caesar.

The third beat is about what the witches said concerning Banquo and me, and again, my phrases focus strictly on this line of thought: "He chid the sisters"; "And bade them speak to him"; "They hail'd him father to a line of kings. Upon my head they plac'd a fruitless crown"; "no son of mine succeeding." Again, the keys follow in the same fashion.

Take a look at the scene score in appendix C. Read over what are marked as the first three beats. Are they marked effectively? Certainly, discerning the story of the beats is fairly simple:

The first beat is about morning greetings.
The second beat is about whether the neighbors are home.
The third beat is about what Goldie knows concerning the neighbors.

Are these beats marked correctly? I would argue that they are not. I would argue that the third beat is actually two beats, the first of which is about whether the neighbors' car is in the garage and the second of which is about why Goldie cares about the neighbors. Though you may be able to articulate the story of any given beat in eight words or less, story, like many of the other tools outlined herein, will only take you so far. Acting is a living thing and, like many living things, resists being broken down into component parts. Mistakes are easily made.

However, using story as a tool will help you check your beats and focus your choices and, in the end, can serve to point you straight toward the core of any given beat. Using story can, in fact, point you straight toward the very core of a play. For instance, what is the story of *Hamlet*, in the fewest words possible? How about this: Hamlet avenges his father's death. Five words. From his first moment to his last, that is what Hamlet is pointed toward—avenging his father's death. Can we do it in fewer? Perhaps. Hamlet avenges. Isn't this, in a nutshell, what Hamlet does in the course of the play? Isn't this Hamlet's *action*?

CHAPTER 8

Defining Action

No matter what way you view the situation, Western culture is all-pervasive. While, as I write this, I have never left the continental United States, I've seen, read, and heard enough about other countries to know that the Western cultural influence affects every human being on the face of the planet. In the world of the present, we live under a system, and that system is based on money. Most of us, if not the vast majority of us, worship the almighty dollar. Even if we don't, most of us are forced to focus a large part of our lives on it, and the same can be said, to a great extent, of all people the world over. From the executive to the manager to the waitress to the dishwasher, we sell the hours of our lives to corporations in order to obtain the means of existence.

We live in a culture that values money over life. One need look no further than the reasons that underlie any war, the reasons we blithely accept the extinction of a species or two every day, the reasons we now allow corporations to sell us the very water that we drink because these same corporations have managed to pollute practically every standing body of potable water on the planet, to see the truth of this statement.

Valuing an abstraction over the real makes us turn inward. If we spend our lives competing with each other to gain an abstraction, every other human being becomes an object because every other human being is our competition for the abstraction. In the truest sense possible, every other human being becomes our enemy. In the America of today, we no longer know our neighbors. Most of us don't even *want* to know our neighbors. A stranger, any stranger, no matter his or her race or gender (although, obviously, race and gender have an effect on us when it comes to strangers because, without question, we live in a racist and sexist culture)—any stranger becomes a threat to our well-being, and our well-being goes beyond our simple existence because our existence—our *subsistence*—is based on money.

What does this mean for the actor? *Everything*. This is, in fact, our cultural imperative. In life, we constantly act on others to get the things we want, no matter how altruistic or idealistic we claim our motives to be. The individual who exists only to benefit others is the vast exception to the cultural rule. Because our cultural system is based on money, the obtaining of the commodity also means the obtaining of power and control. If you control the means of subsistence, you control the individuals who seek that subsistence because you possess the thing for which they work.

This competitive aspect of our culture affects everything we do. If you're a man in Western culture, a woman is a conquest, no matter how much we may rhapsodize about true love. Less than a hundred years ago, a woman was a man's chattel, his possession in a very literal sense. To say we've moved beyond this simple fact is to ignore the obvious. If you're a woman in Western culture, a man is a means of obtaining subsistence and support because the world still belongs to men, whether we wish to acknowledge the fact or not. Each of us is motivated by money, and each of us will be until we decide to acknowledge it and eradicate its influence.

Modern acting methods fall right in line with this pervasive cultural influence. Even if a modern acting method focuses on action at a given point, at some point each method requires an actor to turn inward, usually toward emotion, instead of outward, toward others. An actor who plays a lover is supposed to "be in love" with another. "Be in love" implies a state of being, but when we interact with our love interests in our everyday lives—our love *objects*—we don't focus on the fact of our "love." We focus on getting the thing we want, whether it's the object's "love," the object's attention, the object's body, or the object's money. And in order to get the thing we want, we *take action.* We flatter. We charm. We flirt. We seduce. We invite. We entice. Entrap. Beguile. Captivate. Enchant. Lure. Tempt. We *do* things. Certainly, we feel things as we do things, but feeling things will not get us what we want. Only *doing* things gets us what we want. Only *taking action.* Talk is cheap, feelings are cheaper, and actions speak louder than words or emotions.

The actor is the center of the theater, and the theater is about the truth of life. In the theater, an actor is tasked to "play" a character. What is a "character"? In the simplest and most obvious terms I can muster, a character is a human being—chances are a human being just like you—working within a cultural system that is based on competition for an abstraction. In point of fact, the character you play *is* you. Not someone like you. You are the character you play, in the same way that you are yourself. Again, denying this fact is denying the obvious. And just like you, that character is *doing things* within a cultural system in order to obtain the means of existence. If actors wish to bring the truth of life, of human life, to the eyes, ears, minds, and souls of an audience, then actors must find a way to make the truth of life palpable, and the primary way to do this is through the use of action.

It's important to make a distinction between "actions" and "tasks." Certainly, all of us perform many tasks each day. We wash the dishes. We sweep the floor. We drive the car. We shop for groceries. But the tasks we perform always are directed toward an end, a goal, an object. We wash the dishes, sweep the floor, and shop for groceries to please our families. We drive the car to get to the meeting to please our employers. In every instance, the tasks we perform are directed toward an obvious end result, a need, want, desire or goal—an obvious objective.

Action and Objective

A few years ago, action and objective melded together for me. I've found that discussing them separately isn't as conducive to effective acting as simply discussing what a character is doing—what a character's *action* is—and letting objective take care of itself. I used to separate them, in a traditional manner, like this:

- **Objective:** what a character wants
- **Action:** what a character does to get what he wants

Separating them in this way, however, makes action seem secondary, and it isn't. It's *primary. It's what we should throw our concentration toward in performance.* It's a chicken/egg thing. Which comes first? Objective? But, just as an audience can't see our emotions, an audience can't *see* objective. An audience *sees action.* They watch it happen right there in front of them. For an audience, objective is obscure and action is concrete. The reason I no longer place any analytical focus on objective is that it doesn't help actors in a concrete way.

Sometimes, when I'm writing about action, it will seem as if I'm referring to something that is actually an objective. But if it's playable, no matter how you wish to refer to it, it's action. When I'm working with actors, I talk about objective often. But I talk about objective often because, analytically speaking, it's often easier to discern what a character wants than what a character is doing. If you're confused about what a character's action is, then considering what a character wants often can lead you straight to the action you're having trouble discerning. In addition, while an objective is often not playable (for instance, "to make money" is a possible objective, but try playing *that* concretely), objectives exist that *are* playable. So, if you're having difficulty figuring out the action of a character, it can be useful to discern the character's objective and see if it's playable. And in the end, it can be greatly productive. In other words, mixing objective with action doesn't hurt as long as the objective is something that's *playable.*

Playability

When I look up the word "play" in my dictionary, I get approximately three thousand words defining this single word. Rather than type all of the definitions, I'm going to select the definitions of "play" that I believe are useful for an actor:

- An act of briskly handling, using, or plying a sword or other weapon or instrument
- The conduct or carrying on of a game
- A particular act, maneuver, or point in a game
- An act, way, manner, or method of proceeding: MANEUVER, MOVE (There's that "method" word again)
- Free or unimpeded motion
- So as to be engaged or occupied
- In such a condition or position as to be legitimately played: properly in a game: not dead (I like this one for that "not dead" reference. If something onstage is *really* playing, it's definitely "not dead." As opposed to, for instance, what you can find in any number of theatrical productions in any given city, in any given country, on any given evening.)
- To have an effect: operate (Do I need to tell you that this is my favorite so far?)
- To take advantage: make use (I like this one too. In fact, I like all of these, but some more than others.)
- To exert, or seek to exert, wiles or influence
- To move or function freely within prescribed limits
- To conduct oneself in a specified way (Not wholly useless, but probably the weakest of all of them so far.)
- To treat, use, or work upon [a person] for a certain end (I don't have to say this one is right on the money, do I?)
- To carry in execution
- To put in action or motion (Yes, this one. This one in addition to that "treat, use, or work upon" one.)

How about this: to put into action or motion by treating, using, or working upon a person for a certain end.

That's our definition of "playable." (Sounds, not coincidentally, a lot like one of our definitions of acting: doing with a purpose.) Something is "playable" if it puts one into action or motion by treating, using, or working upon another person for a certain end. Keep in mind that we're not defining "action" here. We're defining "playable."

Hierarchy of Effective Playability

Below, I've listed the hierarchy of the elements that contribute to effective playability:

1. Action
2. Objective (if phrased like an action)
3. Analysis
4. Physical qualities
5. Tactile qualities
6. Words that imply physical or tactile qualities

While I believe action and objective are somewhat clear at this point, some of these other elements are new. Playing your analysis is focusing on executing your score effectively. (I realize that I'm jumping ahead just a bit here, as I haven't outlined the presentational tools that are applied to an analysis, but please trust me when I say that an effective analysis, when combined with effective use of the presentational tools, is playable.) "Physical qualities" are words that imply a purely physical action, like push, pull, press, and stroke. "Tactile qualities" are words that imply a physical state of being, like hard, soft, cold, and hot. Some words that imply physical or tactile qualities are nauseous, energized, and concentrated.

Why this arrangement for the hierarchy? Action comes first because action is the be-all and end-all of acting. Objective, if phrased like an action, comes closest to action and therefore comes second. Analysis is third because an analysis, when effectively combined with the presentational tools, will at the very least allow an audience to clearly receive the story. Playing nothing but your analysis will, in many cases, allow you to act effectively. However, in almost every case, solely playing your analysis won't allow you to activate a story effectively, and the ability to activate a story is, or should be, the ultimate goal of any actor.

Attempting to play anything beyond action, objective, and analysis should be approached with the utmost care, because none of those other playable items contains the cerebral component that actions, objectives, and analysis contain. They ignore the mind and concentrate solely on the body. Physical qualities come next because physical things are playable and are almost always directed at an object. Tactile qualities are playable in a physical sense, but they're almost wholly "inner-directed" and therefore lack the "moving outward" that action and, in some cases, objective and physical qualities, contain. I include words that imply physical or tactile qualities because these kinds of words can lead you *concretely* toward something playable, but I seriously question their usefulness. It's almost dangerous to include them on the list, or even mention them. It's always dangerous, and almost always counterproductive, to refer to the "quality" of anything when it comes to acting.

You'll notice that nowhere in this list have I put "states of being" or "emotions," because *they are not playable*. Attempting to play states of being and emotions will lead you only to making faces and otherwise mugging in a physical way. In other words, attempting to play emotions or states of being will make you direct your focus inward, and when we're out there every day, in the "real" world, working on others, we're not focused inward, we're focused *outward*. Acting is work on one's self, but often when you're acting, you're also working on *someone else*.

A bit confusing, perhaps? Actually, I don't think so. Acting has a dual nature. Acting is work on one's self, but when you're acting, you're working on someone else. When you act, you are both yourself and the character you play. When you act, you are both telling the story and a part of the story. If you like, you can see this as a paradox, or you can see it as the nature of the beast, as a part of the fundamental, elemental, universal truth that acting reflects. In a very real sense, acting—the act of live storytelling—is a reflection of the nature of the universe. The universe, after all, also has a dual nature, also is a "paradox": order and chaos. Good and evil. Yin and yang. There is no paradox, really. There is no contradiction. There is only the nature of the thing itself.

Acting effectively is about walking a very fine line. Most acting I see doesn't even fall close to that line, not necessarily through lack of effort, but certainly through lack of understanding. Often, I think it isn't even possible to walk the line, but I do believe it's possible to come close to it, to fall to one side or the other of it. Coming close to it is, in fact, exactly what you should aim for—but you must first locate the line to be walked.

A Definition of Action

Hamlet avenges.

Now, you could say that Hamlet re-venges. If you look up the definitions of the words "avenge" and "revenge," you'll find that they're inextricably linked, because each contains the other as a part of its definition—at least, each did in the dictionary I used. The difference is that "avenge" is a purely transitive verb, whereas "revenge," while being a transitive verb, also has meaning as a noun. For purity's sake, I chose "avenge," as it has meaning only as a transitive verb. And when it comes to action in the theater, transitive verbs—verbs that take not just any object, but in almost every case, a *human* object—are what you seek.

At this point, defining action as precisely as possible may be helpful. When I look up the word "action" in my dictionary, I don't find a single definition that I believe embodies "action" as we use it in this technique, and as I've understood it to be used in every acting method with which I'm familiar, and that's curious. The idea of action in the theater has been around for centuries, and has been clearly postulated as a key to effective acting for decades. Along with emotion, action is a cornerstone of most modern acting theories. Yet there's not a single definition I can find that sums up the idea of action as we use it in the theater. This is the one that comes closest: an operating mechanism.

> **mechanism** 1 : a piece of machinery; also : a process or technique for achieving a result.

A *technique.* For *achieving a result.* Do I need to tell you I like that? The *action* of a gun. What is the "action" of a gun? It's the "feeling" of it, the amount of pressure that it takes to make that hammer work and strike that bullet and fire it through that barrel. Yes, I like that a lot.

Action is the mechanism we use to operate our characters. Before we enter those rooms every day of our lives out there in the "real" world, on some level, conscious or unconscious, we've made a plan, and we enter and execute it. How do we execute it? We *take action.* We've decided on a course of action before we walk through the door, and we enter our rooms and we *go after* the people in there. We *act* upon them. And characters in plays—*people* in plays—do the same thing. They have a plan before they walk into the room and they go in and they *execute the plan.* They *take action.*

CHAPTER 9

Discerning Action

THE FINAL STEP IN ANALYSIS is discerning the actions of your character. When working on your score, you should provide two different types of actions: **main action** and **beat actions**.

Your main action should embody *everything you do* in the course of any given play, and is used to assist you in activating your presentation and in discerning your beat actions. A beat action covers only what you do in any given beat, and is used to assist you in deciding how to manipulate the presentational tools.

Following are the actions I've chosen for the monologue score from *Macbeth* in appendix B. (I include the objects of the beat actions for the sake of clarity.)

- Main Action: to control my fears
- 1st Beat Action: to intrigue (the audience)
- 2nd Beat Action: to alert (the audience)
- 3rd Beat Action: to ignite (the audience)
- 4th Beat Action: to impassion (the audience)
- 5th Beat Action: to invoke (the fates)

Look at the main action—"to control my fears." At first glance, this action may seem inner-directed. However, all of the things Macbeth fears are outside him, so while they are "his" fears, they're separate from him. Therefore, the action is outer-directed, as any effective action should be. Also, discerning and articulating the object of your main action is extremely helpful, although not absolutely necessary. While this type of waffling on my part may be irritating, there's a reason for it: The object of your action is almost always the person to whom you are speaking. However, articulating the object of your action in terms of a group of objects, and giving that group a name, can be helpful, especially when writing a main action.

Does the main action "to control my fears" apply to everything that Macbeth does in the course of the play? Consider Macbeth's first line: "So foul and fair a day I have not seen." As the main action is directed at his fears, every line Macbeth speaks and everything Macbeth does should be directed, in some form or fashion, at his fears. What is it that Macbeth fears in this initial line? At first glance, it may appear that he fears *the weather*, but look beyond that. While some human beings may not fear the unknown and unfamiliar, most do, and it's the unknown and unfamiliar—the uncontrollable—that Macbeth refers to in this line. It's also the unknown and unfamiliar that he attempts to control at many points throughout the course of the play.

When he speaks this particular line, he's speaking to Banquo, so whatever his beat action is, it should be directed at Banquo. Why say this to Banquo? To seek reassurance concerning the state of the weather? But Macbeth can't "seek" Banquo. Keep in mind that a beat action must be directed at the person to whom you are speaking—Macbeth can seek *for* Banquo, but he can't *seek* Banquo. The final test of an effective action should always be to determine if it can be played *right at* its object, and you can do that by determining whether the verb takes the word "you" directly. I can control you. I can intrigue you. I can alert you. I can ignite you. But I can't seek you in the same way I can control, intrigue, alert, and ignite you.

So why make this statement about the weather to Banquo? Using my trusty thesaurus, I find that "assay" (to examine by trial or experiment) is a synonym for the word "seek." While I don't believe "assay" is the most effective action for this beat, I believe it's closer than "seek." Again, using my trusty thesaurus, I find the following synonyms for "assay": appraise, apprise, assess, check, check out, estimate, evaluate, examine, eyeball, inspect, investigate, measure, peg, prove, rate, read, see, size, size up, survey, test, try, valuate, value, weigh.

It might appear, from the above example, that the choices are endless. They are! Isn't that wonderful? Macbeth wishes to control his fears, and he does so by seeking Banquo's assistance. He does, in fact, seek the assistance of many individuals throughout the course of the play in order to perform his main action. When he asks Banquo about the weather, he's testing him (see "test" in that list of choices?), testing Banquo's knowledge of the nature of the universe and its workings. While this might not be the most effective action for this particular beat, it certainly offers an interesting choice, and it was arrived at directly through consideration of Macbeth's main action in the context of the beat.

In the final analysis, the action statement "to control my fears" applies to every action Macbeth takes during the course of the play. From first line to last, and every in-between. As substantiation of this assertion, I can only offer what I've already written and the following lines, all spoken by Macbeth near the end of the play:

> I have almost forgot the taste of fears . . .
> I pull in resolution, and begin
> To doubt the equivocation of the fiend
> That lies like truth: "Fear not, till Birnam wood
> Do come to Dunsinane:" and now a wood
> Comes toward Dunsinane.
> . . . What's he
> That was not born of woman? Such a one
> Am I to fear, or none.
> Thou'lt be afraid to hear it.
> No, nor more fearful.
> Accursed be that tongue that tells me so,
> For it hath cow'd my better part of man!

I'm sure you'll agree that controlling his fears is, at the very least, central to Macbeth's character.

Take another look at the actions I've written for Macbeth's monologue, this time specifically examining the beat actions. Note how each builds on the one previous, and how all relate to the main action. The action articulated for each beat goes directly toward controlling, in a very specific way, the object of the action, and is directed at obtaining something very specific from the object of the action. Most importantly, consider what each of the beat actions implies regarding choices you might make concerning the presentation of the text. Does the word "intrigue" imply a specific set of physical and vocal tactics? Does the word "alert" also imply a specific set of physical and vocal tactics? Are two different sets of tactics implied by the two different words? Do "ignite," "impassion," and "invoke" do the same? An argument could be made that "ignite" and "impassion" are similar, but not the same. Two different actions—two different, though perhaps similar, sets of physical and vocal tactics. If you examine the actions for the scene score in appendix C, you'll find exactly the same qualities in the actions: the outer-directedness of the main action and beat actions, and the relationships that bounce and echo between them.

If you are an actor, your art is in words.

A Method of Discerning Action

As I wrote previously, I love actors. I'd like to say that I love all human beings, but that isn't true. Human beings exist who don't deserve anyone's love. But if you're an actor—if you're compelled to act—I love *you*. For whatever reason, actors feel the need to put themselves on the line in the most personal, most vulnerable way possible. I have tremendous respect and admiration for that compulsion, but at the same time, and as I wrote previously: Actors are *lazy*. Actors hate working hard. Actors want it all to come easy. The rarest actor I meet is the actor who actually comes to work.

But when it comes to action, work you must. Because action isn't easy. Action is difficult. Next to actually playing it, discerning the action of a character is the most arduous thing about acting. However, there's a fairly certain method for discovering the underlying action of a character, and that method involves immersing yourself in the words of the playwright. Sometimes, the action may seem obvious (Hamlet avenges), and in such cases the method I describe below may seem unnecessary and redundant. However, you should utilize it even if you believe you've arrived at an action that embodies your character, if only to check yourself. In any case, by the time you've completed this exercise, you'll know the text of the playwright about as well as it can be known:

1. Obtain an unmarked copy of your script.
2. For each of your lines, go through and circle meaningful phrases and words. Circle anything and everything that you believe is meaningful. For this exercise, you aren't looking for key phrases and key words, but literally anything at all that may be truly meaningful in the text.
3. Once you've circled every phrase and word you believe is important, go through and cross out all phrases and words that don't *excite* you. When I say, "excite," I mean exactly that—cross out anything that doesn't appeal in a visceral way directly to your senses.

As an example, I circled the following phrases and words in a monologue from Harold Pinter's *The Lover*: trapped, husband think, expects, waiting, can't get out, trapped, treat, married woman, think, think, think, doing, forward, husband, understand, husband, understand, come, come, explain, think, marriage, adores, come, come, whisper, whispering, late tea, think, like, sweet, seen, sunset, husband's, late-night conference, look different, wearing, strange suit, tie, take off, jacket, change, change, clothes, change, darling, like. (Note that in most instances, I've circled *verbs*.)

It's obvious that I didn't circle every word in the monologue. Rather, I circled only those words that I found truly meaningful. I then went through the list and crossed out those phrases and words that didn't truly excite me and was left with the following: trapped, can't get out, trapped, married, forward, come, come, marriage, adores, come, come, whisper, whispering, sweet, late-night conference, wearing, take off, change, change, clothes, change, darling.

Given the words above, can you choose a single transitive verb (that takes a human object) that best describes what this character is doing to the person to whom she is speaking? While

I'm certain you can—in fact, I think it's quite obvious—it's at this point that you need to utilize a tool that should become as invaluable to you as your script: a thesaurus. A standard *Roget's Thesaurus* is extremely useful, but, if you have Internet access, an equally useful and more easily manipulated tool is a Web site that contains a thesaurus function. The Web site that many of my workshop participants and I have found most useful is *www.dictionary.com*.

After working your way through your script, choose the verb from your list of words that you believe comes closest to the main action of your character. In this case, I will use the verb "trap," the first verb I encounter in the list. When I look up the word "trap" using the thesaurus option on Dictionary.com, I'm presented with fifty entries. The first is for "entrap," which, although it contains the word "trap," is not the word I'm looking for. The second entry is for the word "trap," but in this case, "trap" is used as a noun. The third entry for the word "trap" is for a verb, and I'm presented with the following synonyms: ambuscade, ambush, bag, beguile, box in, catch, circumvent, collar, corner, corral, deadfall, deceive, decoy, dupe, enmesh, ensnare, entangle, entrap, fool, grab, hook, inveigle, land, mousetrap, nab, nail, net, overtake, rope in, seduce, snag, snare, suck in, surprise, take, tangle, trammel, trip up.

Does any one of these words apply to the list of words I've extracted from the monologue? All are transitive verbs, and with the exception of the most obscure, most imply strong sets of physical and vocal tactics. Almost all take a human object. However, I believe only one is wholly appropriate not just for the set of words I've chosen, but especially given the title of the play, and that word is "seduce."

It's not a matter of *interpretation*. It's a matter of *attempting to see what is actually there*. Here's what's actually there: trapped, married, come, whispering, late-night conference, wearing, take off, change. (I love that "late-night conference" phrase. Whenever I have a "late-night conference," I know exactly what it is I'm doing.)

I realize that I'm being selective, but I believe my selectivity is logical and true to the source. The idea is to support the story the playwright has written, to *see what is actually there*. "Seduce" implies sexuality—strongly, much more strongly than any other verb offered in that list of synonyms. The final set of words at which I arrived also implies sexuality strongly. As does the monologue.

This is what it comes down to: Your action, like every other choice you make, should come straight from the text. It shouldn't be what you want it to be or tend to think it is or guess it might be. It should *be what it is*. And if you don't like that action or you're afraid of that action or you don't want to perform that action—*then you absolutely must do it*. When you feel most safe, that's when you're most in danger. In danger of being pedestrian. Of being run-of-the-mill. Of being deadly. Of being what most theater is.

Clearly understand that, with this particular monologue, I got lucky. The first verb I encountered in the monologue led me in an almost uninterrupted path straight to the verb that was most appropriate to use as a main action. It may very well be that this particular verb isn't effective as a main action for the play as a whole, or even for this monologue in the context of the play, but here I'm not dealing with the play as a whole. I'm dealing with a monologue out of the context of the play, and I must deal with it on its own terms. For any piece, you must deal with it on its own terms. When choosing a verb for a main action, you want one that's general enough to encompass everything you do in a given piece of text—whether for a play, a scene, or a monologue—but specific enough to be useful in an immediate, presentational sense. (If you're interested in reading the entire monologue in *The Lover* from which the above list of words was taken, you can find the play in Pinter's *Complete Works: 2*, published in paperback by Grove Press.)

Human Objects

Let's take a brief look at a verb that you should be very wary of using in a main action because, in some sense, it can be used to describe the action of practically every character ever put to the page. It's the verb I chose to use as Macbeth's main action: to control.

If you go to Dictionary.com, choose the thesaurus option, and type in the word "control," you get this message: "152 entries found for *control*." Finding a verb that has more than 152 entries is a challenge. "Work" only receives 141 entries. "Force," on the other hand, receives 187 entries. (And what does this tell you about the state of our culture?) "Love"—a paltry 82.

Not all transitive verbs are created equal. As with key phrases and key words, some verbs are more important than others. When searching for an action verb, whether for use as a main action or as a beat action, you're looking for a verb that takes an object. But as I've said before, not just any object: in almost every instance, a *human* object.

Take another look at those 152 entries for "control." The first entry, "birth control," functions as a noun, so we'll find no help there. The second entry functions as a verb with the meaning "reign"—now we're on the right track. The first synonym offered in this entry is the word "administer." For our purposes, this is a weak transitive verb because it does not effectively take a human object. If you happen to be using Dictionary.com and look up the definition of "administer," you'll find the following entry:

1. To have charge of; manage
   a. To give or apply in a formal way : *administer the last rites*
   b. To apply as a remedy : *administer a sedative*
   c. To direct the taking of (an oath)
2. To mete out; dispense : *administer justice*
3. To manage or dispose of (a trust or estate) under a will or official appointment
4. To impose, offer, or tender (an oath, for example)

"Administer" is a weak verb because it isn't directed at a human object. The first definition, "to have charge of; manage," is inner-directed and implies a state of being. Certainly "manage" is an effective transitive verb for our purposes, as it means "to direct or control the use of; handle." One can direct or control the use of, or handle, people, but in the case of "administer," "manage" refers to *having* charge of something. While one can certainly "have charge of" people, this sense of the verb doesn't indicate specific action directed toward those people. Even if you were administering the last rites to someone, as is suggested by one of the definitions, your action isn't "to administer"; that's merely your task, and besides, it's directed at an inhuman object—the last rites. When a priest administers the last rites, he is comforting a dying human being. "To comfort" is a much more effective action in such an instance, and implies a much clearer and more playable set of physical and vocal tactics.

Learn to look past the task and see the truth of human behavior.

Some interesting transitive verb choices can be found in that first list for "control." For instance, the fourth and fifth entries, "boss" and "bully," are particularly intriguing. Without question, I can boss you (keeping in mind that the final test of an effective transitive verb is whether or not it can take the word "you" as its direct object). I can bully you as well, and while "boss" and "bully" are similar in meaning, I don't believe anyone would argue that "bully" implies a stronger and more extreme set of physical and vocal tactics than "boss." In fact, off the top of my head, I can think of a variety of characters whose main action could easily be "bully," and my bet is that you can as well. For such a character, you might be tempted to use the verb "control" as a main action. For many characters, you might be tempted to use the verb "control" as a main action because so often we human beings seem to seek exactly that—control over other human lives. Hamlet avenges, but could we also say that Hamlet controls? After all, "control" seems to be a verb that is applicable to a wide range of characters. Macbeth is all about control, right?

Yes, Macbeth is all about control, but Hamlet isn't. Hamlet's lack of control is one of his problems. Circumstances are being imposed on him from the beginning of the play—circumstances that are out of his control. All Hamlet knows is that something is rotten in Denmark, and he believes it has to do with the death of his father. From the beginning of the play to the end, he's working to avenge his father's death. Does the word "avenge" contain the word "control"? Certainly, and there are points in the play where Hamlet does control events—the play within the play being the most obvious. Does the word "avenge" also contain the word "forgive"? Absolutely. Any action you choose also will imply its opposite (there's that dual nature of the universe again), and Hamlet does forgive someone during the course of the play: his mother.

Don't Repeat Yourself

When writing beat actions, you're going to be tempted to repeat yourself. *Don't.* While the list isn't endless, there are a tremendous number of actions available to choose from. You may find similarities between verbs—as there are similarities between "boss" and "bully" and between "compliment" and "seduce." If we humans have coined a word to describe it, any transitive verb will have a meaning all its own and imply a set of physical and vocal tactics all its own. At a beat change, one part of the story ends and another begins. But what *changes?* Your *action*. And your action dictates all the choices you make concerning your physical and vocal tactics—concerning your use of the *presentational tools.* Once chosen, your main action should reflect all the actions you've selected for your beats, and all your choices concerning both your main action and your beat actions should be strongly outer-directed transitive verbs that take very clear *human objects.* Because when we act in life, we don't act alone, in ourselves, by ourselves. We act on *others,* and in extremely different and varying ways.

A Qualitative Difference

One could assert that, by asking you to define action in this way, all I'm really doing is arguing semantics. (Not that there's anything wrong with arguing semantics. If you're an actor, semantics should be the grease for your wheels.) After all, does any real difference exist between "to tantalize" and "be tantalizing?" Yes, there is a difference—a *monumental* difference. If you're thinking the former, you're directing it outward. If you're thinking the latter, you're directing it inward. And with action, outward is what we seek because, in life, we work *outward.* Not much quantitative difference may exist between saying "to tantalize" and "be tantalizing," but there is a huge *qualitative* difference. If you want to change the way you act, you need to change the way you talk about acting, and in order to change the way you talk about acting you must change the way you *think* about acting. You must, in fact, change the way you think about *life.*

CHAPTER 10

Scoring Your Script

AT THIS POINT YOU MAY VERY WELL ASK, "Am I ever going to memorize the lines?" Soon. I promise.

If you're fortunate enough to be cast in a role—*any role*—approach it in the following manner:

1. **Read the script**. Read the *entire* script. After you've read it once, *read it again*. Read it until you're certain you have a fundamental grasp of the story the playwright is telling. You have been tasked to represent a human life. No, more—you have been tasked to represent the *truth* of human life. Writing a play is difficult. Successful playwrights work hard at what they do. They spend tremendous amounts of time creating the lives of their characters. Even if you work your hardest, chances are you won't spend one-tenth the time in preparing your role that the playwright did in preparing the script. Be as true to the words of the playwright as I hope you are true to yourself, for on the stage, yourself is exactly what you are required to be.

2. **Make a copy of the script**. Always ensure that you have an unmarked copy of the script available to you. If you prepare your role in the way that I suggest, a time will inevitably come when you'll want to go back and read a clean copy of the play.

3. **Using a pencil, mark your beats**. Note that I suggest "a pencil." Don't mark your script with a pen or some other type of indelible marker. Keep your score as uncluttered—as simple—as possible. If you mark it with something indelible, in almost every case, you will eventually regret it.

Once you believe you've marked your beats accurately, put the script aside for as long as possible, then go back and check the beats. Chances are excellent that you won't mark the beats correctly the first time. Chances are excellent that, as you work through the rehearsal process, you'll discover beats that you didn't mark. You'll also discover that beats you did mark don't work effectively and, therefore, weren't marked correctly. In every case, you should make adjustments in your score as necessary.

4. **Using your pencil, circle your key phrases.** Begin by circling what you believe is the single most important phrase in each beat, which more than likely will be at or near the beginning of each beat. (For the *Macbeth* monologue, for instance, I would choose, "Our fears in Banquo stick deep," "They hail'd him father to a line of kings," and "If 't be so/for Banquo's issue have I 'fil'd my mind" as the most important phrases in the middle beats.)

After you've circled the single most important phrase in each beat, go back and consider circling other, additional phrases, always keeping in mind that, while most key phrases will be found at or very near the beginning of each beat, some will be found at or toward the end of each beat and some will be found in the middle of each beat. Also keep in mind that, for a monologue, you will circle 35 to 40 percent of the words in your script. I've found this rule to be *absolutely* consistent over a wide range of styles, from the most classic to the most modern. When working on a play or a scene, this rule doesn't hold true for many minor characters, but it does hold true for a major role in any given script.

5. **Using your pencil, underline your key words.** Keep in mind that you'll key approximately one out of eight words. This rule holds true for any character, large or small, in any play or scene, and certainly for any monologue. If you're tempted to key more than one out of eight words, then you're overkeying. If you're tempted to key less than one out of eight words, then you're underkeying.

6. **As a check, go through the script and see if you can discern the story of each beat.** Once you believe you have discerned

the story of a beat (e.g., this beat is about being safe as king; this beat is about my fear of Banquo), review the beat and see if what you've articulated as the story of the beat corresponds with the phrases and words you've chosen to key. In other words, make sure, as much as possible, that you're using the language of the play to tell the story of the beat. Keep in mind that you need to use eight words or less in filling in the blank: "This beat is about _____."

7. **When you believe you have successfully marked the beats, key phrases, and key words, deduce a main action for the play.** Begin by choosing the first verb that comes into your mind (or the first verb you run across in the script that truly excites you) and write this verb at the top of the first page of your score. While the first verb you choose may be effective, chances are it won't be the most effective—but you have to start somewhere.

   Once you've chosen a verb, begin the process of finding other verbs that echo and reflect it. As you use your thesaurus, you'll undoubtedly find a wide variety of verbs that appear to define your character's actions during the course of the play. Whenever you find such a verb, *write it down*. The list you make will come in handy when choosing your beat actions. Continue the process until you're certain you've chosen the single most effective verb to describe the main action of your character. Change your choice as many times as necessary. (That's why you're using that pencil.)

   When you're certain you've chosen the most effective main action for your character, read the script again and see if the verb you've chosen applies to each beat that you read. If you find even a single beat to which the verb you've chosen doesn't apply, then you haven't chosen the most effective verb. Continue working until there is no doubt whatsoever in your mind that you've chosen the most effective verb possible.

8. **When you believe you've arrived at your main action, choose an action for each beat of the score and write the beat action beside its given beat using the list of verbs you found as you worked.** As much as possible, avoid using the same verb twice. If you don't find a verb in your list that

seems to effectively embody any given beat, then it's time to go back to the thesaurus.

When you're finished, you should have a script that looks similar to the sample monologue and scene scores in the appendixes.

Now Memorize the Score

Once you've scored your script, you're ready to memorize, but you don't simply memorize the words—*you memorize the score.* Memorize the score because when you present the text, you'll deliver not only the lines of the playwright, but also the story's beats, as indicators of vocal and physical changes, and the story's key phrases and words, as indicators of vocal changes. The tools you'll use to manipulate the beats, key phrases, and key words are outlined in part 2, "Presentation."

You're Fooling Yourself If You Don't Believe It

Lot of work, huh? Somewhat daunting, perhaps? At first glance, it may be, but it's much simpler in practice than it appears in theory.

You may believe you can get by without doing all this work, and I wouldn't argue that. A lot of actors do, but only because, as I've said before, they're *lazy.* I am, of course, speaking in generalities here. Not all actors, certainly, but most actors are *lazy.* I think that, generally speaking, this is true of most human beings, especially those under the influence of Western culture, but it's particularly true of actors. Actors believe that they will get by with talent, or good looks, or connections. Anything but actually working at what they do. Actors want it all to come easy. I was once an actor (and may be yet again), so I claim intimate familiarity with an actor's mindset. Actors memorize their lines, but only so they barely know them, and when they get up to perform, they paraphrase, stutter, and lose the lines because their heads are squarely in the audience, seeking that seemingly elusive attention and approval. How any self-respecting actor can get up on a stage and lose lines on a consistent basis—and so many do—is beyond me. It's just laziness. You didn't know them to begin with. Or maybe you just don't care. Maybe—no, probably—you think your innate "artistry" or native "talent" will get you by.

And you may be right. It wouldn't surprise me to find that every "experienced" actor has been positively reinforced for his entire bag of tricks. That's how actors end up with bags of tricks—they find something that works for one character in one play, and the director, who most likely has even less craft than the actors, says, "Hey, that's great, that's funny (or sad), that'll make them laugh (or cry, or sigh, or whatever), do that." The actors proceed to use whatever it is for every character in every play and it becomes a trick and they keep it in their bag and *they're in deep trouble* unless someone comes along and says, "Hey, that's just a bag of tricks. Why don't you try working instead of trying to fool me?"

Why don't you? Why don't you really put some care into your craft? Why don't you stop trying to fool the audience? Why don't you stop trying to fool yourselves?

Why don't you?

CHAPTER 11

Playing the Obvious

BEFORE I LEAVE ANALYSIS, I feel compelled to say something about given circumstances. Much is made in acting circles, particularly in academic institutions, about given circumstances. For those of you who perhaps are unfamiliar with the term, "given circumstances" are those circumstances with which the playwright surrounds your character, e.g., time, place, relationships, economic situation, social background, religious preference, and on and on.

Often the playwright will provide only some of these facts, not all of them. Sometimes, depending on what character you're playing, the playwright won't provide any at all. If you go to an institution of higher education and choose theater as your major, you'll inevitably be asked to do an exercise in which you "fill in the blanks" the playwright has left in the given circumstances. For instance, the playwright may provide only the place where the play occurs—a junk shop, for instance—but not the year the play takes place. He may explicitly state the relationships between the three characters who appear on the stage—they're all friends—but won't state the relationships the characters have with other characters only mentioned during the course of the play. In the institution of higher education, you'll be asked to fill in these kinds of blanks; e.g., if the playwright hasn't articulated a job for your character, you'll have to create a job based on the facts the playwright has provided. In a sense, you become a detective, using the circumstantial clues the playwright provides to figure out everything and anything that the playwright hasn't provided about a character.

"Filling In the Blanks" Is a Waste of Time

For the most part, this exercise is little more than busywork. It has little bearing on anything you'll do on the stage. Why, then, do instructors in institutions of higher education over a wide geographic area ask their students to perform this exercise? Well, they've got to give you *something* to do, and since the vast majority of them don't seem capable of helping you arrive at an effective performance technique, they give you busywork. In addition, this particular exercise plays right into the dominant culture, particularly into many forms of theology. Many religions are more interested in what isn't here than in what is, and focus on the importance of life after death—well, on the potential for life after death, since no one has a certain way of knowing if such a thing as life after death exists—instead of focusing on the importance of life itself. We see this dominant cultural norm played out in the objectification of all living things.

The same goes for this particular exercise. By assigning it, instructors ask you to concentrate on what the playwright has *not* provided rather than on what the playwright *has* provided. An argument could be made that the instructor is asking the actor to focus on what *is* there as well as on what *isn't* there, and I would have to admit the truth of that statement. But as long as someone is asking you to focus, even partially, on what *isn't* there, I would assert that your time as an actor is being wasted. How in the wide world can you play something that *isn't* there?

Play What Is Already There

So here is my advice to you: Play what *is* there. Play the obvious. What I mean by that is, if the playwright has named your character Queen of Sheba, it's a good bet that you're a queen. Does that mean you slouch around and speak quietly? That certainly could be, but chances are that's not what you'll see played out in the actions of the character. If you're a queen, that title should indicate a certain physical and vocal approach to everything that you do on the stage. The same can be said if the playwright has made you a mechanic, a cocaine addict, a prince, a nurse, a politician, a mother, a father. What if the playwright has made you a father who is a cocaine addict? Which takes precedence— the father or the cocaine? I think the answer to that question is *obvious*. And it is exactly this that I'm asking you to play.

Far too often, I see actors not playing the obvious. It's almost as if they have paid little attention to what is actually in the playwright's script. Of course, I don't know what these actors are thinking, but it probably has something to do with impressing the audience, the director, their fellow cast members, or their friends. For the most part, actors concentrate on wanting to "look good," whatever that means. This seems to be particularly true for film actors. God forbid a film actor should appear to be physically unattractive in some way. (Mel Gibson in *Braveheart* comes immediately to mind—sure, his clothes were dirty, his hair was stringy, and he was covered in filth, but check out those teeth.) Of course, there are exceptions to this, as there are with practically anything having to do with acting (Robin Wright Penn comes immediately to mind), but for the most part, many actors just want to look good, and story be damned.

You Were Cast for a Reason

All of this is not to say that what hasn't been provided by the playwright isn't important. Sometimes it can be. But the vast majority of the time, it isn't. The chances of an actor being cast in a role that is "against type" are slim to infinitesimal. In other words, if you're cast, you'll be cast because you are "good" or "right" for that particular role. As I'm fond of saying, you already *are* the character that you're playing. If you weren't, you never would've been cast. So the most effective thing you can do once you're cast, the thing that's best for the story you've been tasked to tell, is to analyze and score the script, memorize the lines, find an effective set of actions to play, and go out on the stage and execute. Don't worry about what *isn't* there. Worry, if you have to, about what *is* there, and act accordingly. If you're cast as the Queen of Sheba, but don't feel that you already *are* a queen, figure out a physical and vocal approach that will assist you in presenting the Queen and execute that, along with your analysis and your actions. The playwright provides everything you need to play any given character. If nature hasn't provided you with some of the necessary ingredients, then do the work—there's that word again—and provide them yourself.

PART 2

Presentation

CHAPTER 12

Tempo and Rhythm

AS THE BEAT IS TO ANALYSIS, SO TEMPO IS TO PRESENTATION. Given the nature of theater, I'd rather have an actor who speaks too loudly than too softly. I'd also rather have an actor who speaks too quickly than too slowly. Speaking too slowly has been the death of many a Shakespeare production for two primary, and quite mistaken, reasons: (1) The idea that Shakespeare is sacred text and therefore must be approached with reverence; and (2) The idea that if you take a lot of time saying all the lines, the audience will be able to better understand them. Both of these ideas are mistaken, and the former is so ingrained in some actors as to be almost unconquerable. Shakespeare was a storyteller like any other storyteller— well, perhaps not like any other storyteller—but his stories, when analyzed, are just like any other stories. Some great stories, some genius stories, certainly, but still only stories all the same. And just because you take time with a line of Shakespeare doesn't necessarily mean the audience will be better able to understand what you're saying. In fact, if you hit a slow tempo and stick to it unbendingly, unchangeably, then you will do nothing for the audience except allow them time to nap.

But I'm getting ahead of myself—an easy thing to do when discussing acting.

Defining Tempo

> **tempo** I : rate of rhythmic recurrence or movement . . . 2 : rate
> of motion or activity : PACE.

"Tempo," as we will refer to it in this technique, is commonly
referred to in many theatrical circles as "pace." My preference is to
use the word "tempo" because tempo is more musically inclined.
In addition, "rhythm," another musically inclined term, is part of
the definition of tempo, which is not the case with "pace."

The Rules of Tempo

Utilization of tempo can be reduced to eight fairly simple rules:

- As you're speaking, you may speak more quickly
- As you're speaking, you may speak more slowly
- You can stop speaking
- You're probably going to be required to speak more slowly
  than usual at the beginning of a scene or a beat
- You're probably going to be required to speak more slowly
  than usual at the end of a scene or a beat
- You're probably going to be required to speak more slowly
  than usual when saying key phrases
- You may speak more slowly than usual when saying a key
  word (In other words, you might not just change the vocal
  stress on a key word as compared to other words you're saying, but you might actually speak more slowly than usual
  when saying it)
- You're probably going to speak more quickly than usual the
  closer you come to the end of a beat (In other words, you're
  going to "drive through"—gradually increase the tempo—
  in any given beat)

You might be surprised that I actually went to the trouble of
writing all that down. To those of you with any kind of experience in the craft, all that may seem obvious. I think most of it
is obvious, but if any of it's obvious, why is it that so many

theatrical productions seem to lack any sense of the above-delineated rules? None of them, of course, are hard-and-fast rules (that's why I've got all those "probablys" in there), but if acting is effective, the tempo of a monologue, a scene, or a play falls right in line with the rules outlined above.

Defining Rhythm

Rhythm is inextricably linked with tempo, and for good reason: The rhythm of a piece is established, to a great extent, by the manipulation of tempo. Tempo and rhythm, like lovers, walk hand in hand. I've looked at a lot of definitions of the word "rhythm," but there's only one that I believe gets to the heart of theatrical rhythm, and it's a long one:

> **rhythm** 2 : an ordered recurrent alternation of strong and weak elements in the flow of sound and silence in speech including the grouping of weaker elements around stronger, the distribution and relative disposition of strong and weak elements, and the general quantitative relations of these elements and their combinations.

Sounds not unlike the rules of tempo and analysis I've outlined so far, i.e., some phrases are more important than others ("strong and weak elements"), and these tend to group themselves ("recurrent alternation" and "distribution and relative disposition") around beat changes ("sound and silence").

What dictates tempo? Mostly, where the beats change.

What dictates rhythm? Lots of different things: the language of a piece; where the beats change; key phrases; key words; pauses, long pauses, silences, and other types of caesuras; and punctuation.

As you may notice, the definition for tempo is very short compared to that for rhythm, and when you consider what dictates tempo, the answer also is short and simple, whereas the answer for what dictates rhythm is considerably longer and more complicated. And I think that's a good indication of how they work together. The idea of tempo *is* simple, really. It's the *manipulation* of tempo that's somewhat complicated, and that's where rhythm comes in—and what makes discussing the rhythm of a theater piece so complicated as to be almost counterproductive. While both tempo and rhythm are tools, the one that is most easily understood is tempo. Rhythm is much more ephemeral, and thus, much more difficult to consider and to manipulate as a tool. Also, though an actor, in an ultimate sense, is the person in control of the tempo and rhythm, the actor doesn't truly dictate either (or at least, the actor shouldn't)—the playwright does. What an actor does with analysis is ferret out the rhythm and tempo that the playwright intends for a given text. Then, when delivering that text, the actor makes the rhythm the playwright provides palpable through the way he manipulates tempo.

Looking at it in another way might be productive. Tempo is speed. Rhythm is the variation of speed. You can control both and discuss both, but only tempo works according to anything like a set of rules. Rhythm is situation-specific. Rhythm depends totally upon the given text with which you're dealing. There are no "rules of rhythm" that can be set down.

Well, on second thought, there may be a couple. Possibly.

The "Rules" of Rhythm

Bear with me. We're going to be treading on some dangerous ground here.

The playwright gives us indicators of rhythm in the text. As mentioned above, some of these indicators of rhythm are the same things we use as indicators of tempo—for instance, the beat changes. At the risk of getting ahead of myself, at any given beat change you're going to "be still," if only for the slightest moment, both vocally and physically. This stillness at beat changes affects rhythm. In a sense, stillness is the rhythm. The playwright also uses punctuation to indicate rhythm, which, of course, includes periods, commas, semicolons, colons, dashes, parentheses, ellipses, quotations, slashes, and any other types of punctuation I've neglected to mention. But be careful: While you can trust the punctuation in modern texts, the older the text is, the more untrustworthy the punctuation.

As an example, a tremendous amount of speculation centers on how Shakespeare intended to punctuate his texts. No method exists of discerning precisely how he punctuated his texts, because we have so few samples of his handwriting and because it has been conclusively shown that so many of his published texts contain typographical errors. Modern plays, however, are different. The playwright has placed and approved all, or at the very least almost all, of the punctuation found in a modern text. You can "trust" the punctuation in a modern text and use it as a source for rhythm.

Along with beat changes and punctuation, playwrights provide another way of indicating rhythm: caesuras (pauses, long pauses, silences, and the like). It has recently become fashionable for playwrights to use another silence indicator (and this ought to really confuse you), indicating a type of silence by using the word "beat," usually placing it in parentheses and leaving it stylishly uncapitalized. Given the way I've seen "beat" used in this context, when a playwright uses the word "beat" as a silence indicator, rather than indicating a "beat change," the playwright seems to be indicating more of what I commonly refer to as a "hitch," which is a kind of silence, but a short one. Actually, given my limited experience with the caesura "beat," I would postulate that it's meant to be slightly longer than a "hitch," but slightly shorter than a "pause." Also, I think it's helpful to think of silence indicators in this way: A "beat" is a very, very short silence; a "pause" is slightly longer than a "beat"; a "long pause" is slightly longer than a "pause"; a "silence" is slightly longer than a "long pause"; and a "long silence" is slightly longer than a "silence."

One last rhythm indicator is actually the most important one: *language*. Language is, of course, situation-specific, and so, barring the pure nature of grammar, is difficult to break down into a set of rules that would be useful for an actor. Some specific instances of rhythmic language use are, however, important to recognize.

In many instances, Shakespeare and his contemporaries wrote in verse. More specifically, they wrote in iambic pentameter, which is a line of dialogue that consists of ten syllables—five sets of two syllables each, with the second syllable in each set receiving stress. In other words, a line of iambic pentameter, rhythmically speaking, reads like this: da-DA da-DA da-DA da-DA da-DA ("the QUA-li-TY of MER-cy IS not STRAIN'D"). While this concept may sound burdensome and repetitious, iambic pentameter can be quite helpful when delivering Shakespearean text—but it also can be quite dangerous if overused because, if everything weighs the same, everything weighs nothing. There are directors who are so focused on iambic pentameter that they completely miss the story and have actors memorize the dialogue with the meter firmly in the forefront of their thinking, ending up with actors delivering all the text da-DA da-DA da-DA da-DA da-DA. While it's true that this strong rhythm can be extremely helpful—sometimes, particularly in Shakespeare, the rhythm *is* the meaning—you should avoid working with these kinds of directors. You, and the play you're performing, will die a truly horrible death.

In addition, there are other patterns in language that can help you recognize what kind of rhythm or tempo you should employ. Basically, they all revolve around the idea of *repetition*. That is, sounds, words, or phrases are repeated in close conjunction with each other. When I say "sounds," I'm referring to alliteration ("the repetition of the same sounds or of the same kinds of sounds at the beginnings of words or in stressed syllables"), which, if highlighted vocally, can be used to powerful effect. When I say "repetition of words and/or phrases," I'm referring to almost any contemporary playwright (go back to the chapter on "Action" and review the words I selected from Pinter's *The Lover*, which contains a tremendous amount of repetition), but you can find such repetition in classic texts as well (check the *Macbeth* monologue in appendix B). If you find such repetition in a text, it's a good sign that the playwright meant for you to deliver the lines that contain the repetition with a quick tempo, because as with rhythm, *the repetition is the meaning*. Again, this is not a hard-and-fast rule, but it's close. You don't need to take time with sounds, words, or phrases that repeat themselves because *the effect is cumulative*. I'm so certain of this that I believe we can postulate it as a rule.

The Rule of Repetition

If you find repetitive words or phrases grouped closely together in a text, chances are the lines that contain such repetitive words or phrases should be delivered with a quick tempo (driven through), because the effect of such groupings is cumulative. The repetition *is* the meaning.

Adjunct to the Rule of Repetition: The Rule of Lists

If you find a list of things in a text, the text that contains such a list should be driven through, because the effect is cumulative. The list *is* the meaning.

Neither of the above-delineated rules is meant to imply that you'll never circle an item in a list or that you'll never circle a word or phrase that repeats itself. On the contrary, chances are excellent that, in the case of a repeating phrase, one instance of the repetitious phrase will be circled, usually the first instance of the phrase. But sometimes the second instance will also be circled if it falls at the end of a beat. In addition, if a list is quite long, you'll probably circle an item or two in the list just to break up the tempo and offer vocal variety to the collective ear of the audience. But generally speaking, the above-delineated rules apply, with little deviation, to every text you'll encounter.

Utilizing Tempo

A beat may begin slowly, then immediately build, and never cease building until its climax. A beat may begin very quickly, then slow, then build quickly again, slow, build quickly again, slow, then build quickly and climax. A beat may begin slowly, get slower, then get slower still, and even slower still, until it fades away to nothing. Tempo patterns are almost as varied as the playwrights who write them and the actors who deliver them, but fortunately, as with so many other elements of the craft, a flexible rule—well, more of a pattern, actually—can be postulated concerning the use of tempo.

The General Tempo Pattern of a Beat

Slow, faster and faster, slow, stop.

As stated above, tempo patterns can be extremely varied, but most beats will start slowly, build to a climax, and then slow and/or stop. While it may not seem so at first glance, if you look at the three tempo patterns I describe above, you can see that the first two (the one that begins slowly, then builds quickly and climaxes, and the one that begins slowly, then builds, slows, builds, etc.) work in a broad sense according to the general tempo pattern of slow, faster and faster, slow, stop. The third beat described, instead of building up, builds *down*, but such a build is the natural antithesis of the general tempo structure of a beat, the natural complement of it, and yet again a reflection of the dual nature of acting. Most beats build *up*. Some beats build *down*. Order and chaos. Good and evil. Yin and yang. Or, more specifically still: orderchaos; goodevil; yinyang.

Relativity

What, precisely, does all this mean in terms of performance? Simply this: You use your score to structure the tempo, and thus establish the rhythm of any given piece. At the beginning of a beat—at the point of *exposition*—chances are excellent that you've circled the first phrase, so your tempo as you deliver this key phrase will be relatively slow. Once you've delivered this initial key phrase and subsequently encounter uncircled material, your tempo should immediately increase *relative to* the tempo you've established, and drive through (*building action*) to the next key phrase. In other words, the tempo of the piece *increases* and *builds* as you deliver the uncircled material. When you encounter another key phrase, the pattern repeats itself: Your tempo decreases *relative to the build* as you deliver the key phrase. Once you've delivered the second key phrase (or third, or fourth, etc.), you increase the tempo of uncircled material in a relative fashion and build again to the next key phrase or to the end of the beat.

If everything weighs the same, everything weighs nothing. Some phrases are more important than other phrases, and the most effective way to draw the ears and minds of an audience to what's important in a text is through the use of tempo. Whenever you slow the tempo of a phrase *relative to* the tempo of the phrases that surround it, that phrase will *pop* out at the listener, because slowing the tempo provides an aural cue for the listener. It lets the listener know that what you're saying is important relative to the rest of what you're saying.

You could go too far with this idea. When I say "slow the tempo," I don't mean slow it down to the speed of molasses. While phrases exist that need to be delivered in an *extremely* slow fashion, they are the exceptions. For instance, in the *Macbeth* monologue I have circled the entire first beat. I suggest that the words that make up that beat be delivered slowly and evenly, not deadly slow. In an attempt to represent it visually: We're looking for, "To be thus is nothing, but to be safely thus," not for, "To—be—thus—is—nothing, but—to—be—safely—thus." Observing the other side of the coin, we're not looking for "Tobethusisnothing, buttobesafelythus." All effective acting walks a fine line.

Tempo works in a *relative* manner. All the presentational tools work in a relative manner. If you're delivering a piece of text using a fairly quick tempo, you don't have to slow circled material a lot to make it pop from the text; rather, you slow circled material *relative to* the tempo that surrounds such material.

The Primacy of Tempo

Tempo is the major presentational tool of the actor, and also works in a manner more consistent than all of the other presentational tools. The use of tempo in any given piece is easily understood because its use directly relates to the intent of the playwright, which you've uncovered in your score by discerning beats, key phrases, and key words. Along with language, the effective manipulation of tempo creates the basic rhythm of a piece. If you're watching a live performance and what you're watching doesn't seem to have any rhythm, this most likely is because the actors are not manipulating tempo effectively.

Every piece of text has its own unique tempo. I'm not writing about whole plays here. I'm writing about *pieces of text*. For instance, if your beat action is to hypnotize someone, you will use a relatively slow tempo. If your beat action is to pressure someone, you will use a relatively quick tempo. (And hopefully, by using these two examples, I am also making it clear how your beat actions affect your vocal presentational choices.) In any case, as for tempo, I'd rather have an actor who goes too quickly than one who goes too slowly. Actually, I'd rather have an actor who goes at just the right speed, each and every time.

CHAPTER 13

Volume and Intensity

VOLUME AND INTENSITY ARE THE TWO OTHER MAJOR VOCAL TOOLS at the actor's disposal. You could say that volume is actually more important than tempo because, if you lack sufficient volume in presenting a text, the audience can't hear, and thus, can't enjoy the play. However, I think I've covered the need for adequate volume in discussing the actor's most basic tools—the mind and the voice—and besides, when it comes to presentation, while the effective *manipulation* of volume is important, it isn't nearly as important as the effective manipulation of tempo.

It's easy to become confused when discussing volume and intensity, as they're so closely linked, but there's little question that they're two different tools. Volume is something that an actor uses and manipulates constantly. Intensity is a situation-specific tool that should be used sparingly. While it's certainly possible to have too much volume and too much intensity, the tool that's most commonly misused is volume. Intensity seldom enters an actor's performance at all, not because it isn't necessary and/or useful, but because most actors don't even seem to be aware of its possible use.

Defining Volume and Intensity

For our purposes, we'll define volume as "a quantity or power of sound," and we'll define intensity as "the force or energy of sound." While at first glance this may seem somewhat confusing, in practice it becomes clear. Saying something quietly doesn't mean that it can't have intensity. For example, if you're seducing someone, you'll most likely be speaking relatively softly, but what you say will have intensity on some level. But if you're flattering someone, what you say will have more volume but less intensity; most likely, it will lack intensity. In a sense, seduction contains a threat, but flattery doesn't, and it's the threat inherent in seduction that warrants the use of intensity.

Manipulation of Volume

As a tool, volume works very much like tempo. At the beginning of a beat, volume will most likely be at its lowest overall point, and as you move through a beat, volume will increase in a relative fashion, sometimes only slightly, sometimes quite radically, depending on the nature of the beat. Chances are the longer the beat, the more the overall volume will increase. For example, here's the second beat of the *Macbeth* monologue:

> Our <u>fears</u> in Banquo stick <u>deep</u>,
> And in his royalty of nature reigns that
> Which <u>would</u> be fear'd. **'Tis much he dares**,
> And to that dauntless temper of his mind,
> He hath a <u>wisdom</u> that doth <u>guide</u> his valor
> To act in <u>safety</u>. **There is none but <u>he</u>**
> **Whose being I do <u>fear</u>**, and under him
> My genius is <u>rebuk'd</u>, as it is said
> Marc Antony's was by <u>Caesar</u>.

If I were presenting this monologue, in this beat the volume would increase in concert with the tempo; as the tempo increased—as I drove through the beat—the volume also would increase.

Over the course of a beat, volume, generally speaking, works very much like tempo. However, volume works in an even more specific way when keying words within a beat. If a word within a beat has been selected as a key word, it will receive increased volume relative to the words that surround it, with primary keys receiving the most volume and secondary keys receiving slightly less. Many actors refer to keying words as "stressing" words. Writers key words by *italicizing* them (like I just did!). Go back and read that last sentence again. Whenever I see an italicized word in a text, I know that if I'm reading it out loud, I'm going to increase my volume when I read the italicized word in order to "stress" it and remain true to the intent of the writer. That's exactly what keying words is all about. (However, when I'm reading a text out loud and I find two or more italicized words in a row, I find that I most often slow their tempo while only stressing one of them, which further highlights the idea that you *slow key phrases* and *increase the volume* of key words. For instance, if you were to read the preceding sentence out loud, my bet is that you would not slow your tempo much, if at all, when encountering the word "slow," but would only increase its volume; however, for the phrase "increase the volume," you would slow its tempo and stress the word "volume.")

Just as an actor's tempo should slow in a relative fashion when encountering a key phrase, a similar pattern should occur in the use of volume. That is, the volume of a key phrase within a beat will lessen *relative to* the volume that has been established. Once the key phrase has been delivered, the volume, like the tempo, will most often pick up where it left off and continue to build. This is exactly the way I believe the second beat of the *Macbeth* monologue should work. The tempo and volume should be at their lowest point in the first phrase of the beat ("Our fears in Banquo stick deep"), with "fears" and "deep," as they are key words, receiving slightly more volume relative to the overall volume. The overall tempo and volume begin to build for the next line and a half, pulling back slightly in a relative fashion for the phrase, "'Tis much he dares," and then continuing to build, with any key words receiving slightly more volume relative to the overall volume that has been established. Again, the tempo and volume will decrease in a relative manner for the phrase, "There is none but he whose being I do fear," and then continue their build, with the word "rebuk'd" receiving more volume relative to the overall volume, as "rebuk'd" is both a key word and, more importantly, the climax of the beat.

Also, because "rebuk'd" is the climax of the beat, either the tempo or the volume, or both, will most likely decrease, if only ever so slightly, for the phrase "as it is said Marc Antony's was by Caesar," since this phrase is the denouement of the beat. It is, in fact, the end of the beat, and you should always consider pulling back the tempo and volume at the end of a beat because this reduction of tempo and volume is a cue for the listener. It lets the listener know that you've made your point and that it is now the listener's turn to speak. Recall that very often, you'll circle the last phrase in a beat, which indicates a reduction in tempo— but this isn't always the case. In other words, you won't always circle the phrase at the end of a beat. You should, however, always consider decreasing the tempo at the end of a beat, whether you've circled the ending phrase or not, if for no other reason than to provide that aural cue for the audience that one part of the story is ending and another is beginning.

Again, I hope you can see that the microcosm (the beat) reflects the macrocosm (the play), with the "exposition/building action/climax/denouement" story structure present in the smaller structure of the beat. If considered closely, the common four-part story structure, and the common tempo-volume pattern that occurs within it, reflect the progress of a human life. First we learn to crawl, which is a slow process; then we learn to walk, and our tempo picks up the more capable we become; then we learn to run; and, if we're fortunate, we live long, our bodies give out, our tempo slows, and we die. I don't believe this is mere coincidence. Storytelling is about the truth of life, so finding the general pattern of a human life reflected in both the inert structure of a story on the page and the living structure of a story on the stage is more than synchronistic; it is harmony and beauty of the highest order.

While most beats work exactly according to this volume pattern, some don't. For instance, in the first beat of the *Macbeth* monologue, which consists of the single line, "To be thus is nothing,/But to be safely thus," chances are as you deliver the line, your overall volume will remain quite even while the tempo increases, if only ever so slightly. The reason for this is that there simply isn't time within such a short beat to increase the volume significantly without sounding anything but insane, and this makes perfect sense. A sure sign of instability is a person who gets loud very suddenly. The only significant change in volume in the first beat of the *Macbeth* monologue comes on the key word "safely," for which you would increase your volume in order to stress—key—the word. The same thing will happen, to a lesser degree, on the secondary keys, but the word that will receive the most stress—the most *volume*—will be the word "safely," as this word is the climax of the beat. This will almost always be the case: The climax of a beat will receive the most volume.

As for tempo and volume, the remaining beats in the *Macbeth* monologue work in the same way as the second beat. It's important to note that the relativity of the presentational tools holds true as well; if you're decreasing tempo, you're always decreasing it relative to the tempo that has been established, and the same goes for volume. As with any monologue, the *Macbeth* monologue is a self-contained scene, a little story, and while the beats each have a climax, there's only one true climax in the monologue if it's considered as a whole. As with all story climaxes, it comes near the end of the monologue—in this case, on the phrase "the seeds of Banquo kings." Everything in the monologue builds to this phrase, so once the tempo and volume begin to build, while they may ebb and flow, chances are they won't return to the form they took in the first beat until the beginning of the next major turning point in the story.

Utilizing too much volume for any given piece of text is a distinct possibility. One of the "rules" of acting I learned when I was very young is that, as an actor, you should never "top out." You should never use all the volume you can muster because you'll leave yourself with nowhere to go. Keeping something in reserve, vocally speaking, is important to bear in mind because if you should top out, you'll end up on one level. And if everything weighs the same, everything weighs nothing. Also, be careful of getting too loud too soon. If you've identified a line or phrase as being important enough to receive a considerable amount of volume, you need to be careful about the way you build to it, for the same reasons that you want to avoid topping out: If you utilize a considerable amount of volume on the lines that precede the important line or phrase you've chosen, then that important line or phrase won't pop out of the text effectively, and you'll undermine your storytelling.

Manipulation of Intensity

Intensity is situation-specific and should be used sparingly and carefully. While there are long pieces of text in existence that deserve to be delivered with tremendous intensity, they're few and far between. You should save intensity for very specific moments that are of paramount importance in the life of a character—in other words, moments in which the character's stakes are the highest. Most often, the moments in which you'll utilize intensity will come only on a single line or, even more often, on a single phrase or word.

In the *Macbeth* monologue, I suggest that if there is a single moment where intensity should be utilized, it doesn't come until the line "If 't be so, for Banquo's issue have I 'fil'd my mind." In other words, the tempo of that phrase will slow and the volume will decrease in a relative way, as it's both the beginning of the beat and a key phrase, but because I'd wish to draw even more attention to this phrase than usual, I would add intensity. I choose to add it here both because it's the beginning of the beat that contains the climax and because Macbeth is realizing something. As soon as I deliver that phrase, I would drop the intensity out and pick up the tempo and volume as I drive to the next key phrase, "and mine eternal jewel." I wouldn't utilize intensity again until the climactic phrase "the seeds of Banquo kings," which, because it's the climax, should receive more volume and intensity than anything else in the monologue. Be careful, though: Just because something is the climax of a beat doesn't necessarily mean it receives intensity. Again, intensity is situation-specific. I believe intensity is required at the two points I have mentioned in the *Macbeth* monologue because the monologue is a turning point in the play for Macbeth. He's making his decision to murder Banquo. For me, that's a situation deserving of the tool.

As you might have guessed from the above, volume and intensity, like tempo, work according to a set of general rules. In fact, these three tools work very much together to allow you to build tension effectively, for what builds during the building action of a story *is* tension, and—reiterating the magic words "macrocosm" and "microcosm"—what builds during the building action of a beat is also tension. Storytelling lives on the creation and release of tension, and the effective use of tempo, volume, and intensity will go far in allowing you to manipulate this storytelling life force effectively.

The Rules of Builds

There are three primary vocal tools to assist you in building tension in a beat: Tempo, Volume, and Intensity. You may use one, two, or all three in any given build, but the one you will use most often will be *tempo*. The following are *very general* rules:

1. At the beginning of a beat, you will deliver the text slowly and evenly (understanding that "slowly and evenly" are relative to any given beat), *especially* if the phrase at the beginning of the beat is circled.

2. As you move into the body of any given beat, depending on its length, most likely you are going to drive the tempo (that is, increase the speed at which you deliver the text) and increase the volume.

3. When you encounter a key phrase within a beat, you'll slow the tempo and decrease the volume *relative to* the tempo and volume that you established when you delivered the uncircled material. Once you've delivered the key phrase and encounter uncircled material, the tempo and volume will increase and build *relative to* the tempo and volume utilized in the key phrase.

4. When delivering a key word, most often you will increase its volume.

5. When driving the tempo and increasing the volume through a beat, the closer you come to the end of the beat, the quicker the tempo will drive and the more the volume will increase.

6. When driving the tempo and increasing the volume during a beat, you are always building to a "climax."

7. When you reach the climax of a beat, chances are excellent that you will decrease the tempo but increase the volume.

8. After the climax has been delivered, the tempo and the volume will decrease (build down) until you get to the beat change. This "build down" in the tempo and volume will usually occur *very quickly*, if at all. Often, a beat will climax at a beat change, so instead of building down, you will simply go still (cease all movement) at the end of the beat.

9. As for intensity, it is situation-specific and should be used sparingly and carefully. An entire monologue might require an intense edge, or only a single word. It depends on the importance of the passage or the word in the story.

Because so many variables are involved here, I attempted to make the above rules as specific as possible. Please understand that most of them are actually *very general rules*. Despite their general nature, especially with regards to tempo and volume, the above rules will more than likely apply to 75 percent of any text you're asked to deliver, and, in some form, to 99 percent.

Your use of the three primary vocal tools in structuring builds should be guided by the analysis you did in your score. While I've written nothing about movement up to this point, movement is actually the simplest of all the presentational tools because it is, in a sense, the least utilized. The most important presentational tools in an actor's box are the three tools I've outlined above: tempo, volume, and intensity. And the effective manipulation of these three tools, like the utilization of movement, is dictated entirely by the form of the score.

Commit to Your Choices

Of paramount importance in effective acting is committing to the choices you make. There are acting teachers who will inform you that acting is all about the choices that you make, and I'd put myself in that category. Unfortunately, most acting teachers will also tell you that the choices you make center around emotion or subtext or some other uncontrollable and/or nonexistent tool, and in this I would disagree—vehemently. All the choices you make should be based on the text you have been tasked to present, not on your desire to emotionally indulge, or on extra-textual information that you create, and all the choices you make should center on the use of things you can control and manipulate, like the analytical and presentational tools outlined herein.

When I say "commit to the choices you make," I mean exactly that. If you've chosen a key phrase, *slow its tempo* relative to the phrases that surround it. *Really* slow it, so that the difference in tempo is noticeable. If you've chosen to key a word, don't just pay lip service to keying it—*key* it. Increase its volume relative to the words that surround it.

Committing to your choices in the way I suggest is of more importance the further dramatic literature moves back in time. Not that I ever would advocate sloppiness, but the collective ear of the audience receives a modern text more easily than a premodern text, so a certain amount of sloppiness in your commitment is more acceptable when delivering more modern material. But with premodern texts, such as Shakespeare's, committing to your choices becomes much more important. *Really* slowing something, *really* keying a word, and *really* driving the tempo of non-key phrases are elements lacking in almost every performance of Shakespeare, or any other premodern play, that I see. And when I see a premodern play working, it's working primarily because the actors, either through conscious craft or through talent and intuition, are really committing to what's important in the text.

I'm tempted to write something about "feeling" tempo and rhythm, and even volume, but that's just ephemera. While I believe an actor who has a complete understanding of the craft can "feel" when the vocal presentational tools are working, no actor needs intuition to guide the use of these tools because these tools can be manipulated *concretely*. No actor has to depend on ephemera when utilizing the tools of the craft, which is why, once you're certain you've established effective manipulation of the vocal presentational tools, you should *set your choices*. Don't change them. Don't imagine that other choices will be more effective. Don't second-guess yourself and, whatever you do, don't allow yourself to *indulge* in your favorite moments. So often, even the most effective actor will change, for instance, a tempo that has been working because, on some level, she wants to indulge in her character's "high" moments—that is, in her character's most important, usually emotional, moments. Actors lose sight of what got them to an effective playing level and begin to indulge their worst instincts for "performance" instead of committing to the sound, text-based choices they made while utilizing their knowledge of storytelling.

I've seen it happen time and again, and it doesn't have to happen. It *shouldn't* happen. While it takes much more work, much more *commitment* on your part, to ensure that you remain consistent when you know something is working and to ensure that you avoid letting your ego take control of your performance. In the end, that kind of commitment to story is worth the effort because it leads you to a consistency of play that is irreplaceable for you, for your fellow actors, and most importantly, for the audience that comes to hear and see your story. If there's a "better" way to deliver the text, it should be crafted long before an audience arrives. Otherwise, you're depending on the audience to "inspire" your presentation. How sound a method is that?

CHAPTER 14

Movement and Stillness

FOR OUR PURPOSES, MOVEMENT IS ANY MOTION the body can make. Stillness is the cessation of movement, and probably the most underutilized, and possibly the most unrecognized, tool in acting. Stillness is, or should be, an actor's physical base, because the effective manipulation of stillness is what holds, and releases, tension in a story.

Storytelling in the theater lives on dramatic tension, on, to quote another dictionary definition, "the act or process of stretching something tight." The four-part pattern of storytelling is a clear indication of the tension inherent in an effectively told story, and this storytelling pattern is echoed in the structure of the beat: If delivered effectively, every beat creates, then releases, tension, and each beat that follows repeats this pattern. Together, in different combinations, the beats make up the larger parts of the story—the scene, the act, the play—which stretch the audience tight, until, finally, they are released.

The effective manipulation of tension in a story is handled primarily through the use of movement and stillness. Keep in mind that when I write "movement," I'm referring to any type of motion the body can make, including the act of speaking. Speaking is movement. When you use the vocal tools, you are moving. Any other physical movements you choose to make are secondary to the primary movement of speaking.

The Nature of Movement in Theater

While the ability to move well and gracefully, to have complete control over all parts of your physical instrument, is a valuable thing for an actor to possess, the ability to move effectively on the stage is vastly overrated. Actors who are in no way in touch with their own bodies can deliver perfectly adequate performances—provided, of course, that they have loud, clear voices. An actor's voice is the center of everything he does, and whenever an actor is speaking, an actor is moving. If he is delivering text effectively, he is moving in a way that creates tension because he is reflecting the four-part structure of storytelling, which is, in a sense, a tension-filled pattern.

Because the four-part structure of storytelling is manifested primarily in the use of the vocal tools, particularly in the use of tempo, all other physical movement should be strictly limited to what will support the story. It is to an actor's advantage to limit it. Because the nature of vocally delivering text requires constant movement of the speaking instrument, if actors also constantly move in an extra-vocal way, then the story is weighted down with movement. The audience cannot see the most essential movement—the delivery of the text—through the mass of the other, extraneous physical movement. The primary movement of the vocal instrument of an actor is a forceful indicator of the need for stillness as an actor's physical base.

The Importance of Stillness

While extra-vocal movement can help manipulate tension in a story by the way it ebbs and flows, it can't hold tension. In order to tell stories effectively, an actor must have a technique not just of creating and building tension, but also of holding, or sustaining, tension. Physical stillness is the key.

Every story begins and ends in stillness, and, as mentioned previously, so should every beat, if only for the slightest moment. When a story is working in the theater, any tension created by an actor within a beat holds when the actor goes still at the beat change, and then releases as the actor moves to begin a new beat. Because the stillness at the beat change allows the tension to hold for the actor, the tension also holds for the audience. In a sense, it allows the audience, if only briefly, to wonder, "What comes next?" If a story is working in the theater, an audience will mirror this pattern precisely: At a moment of stillness, they'll be still as well, and when an actor moves to begin the next beat, they'll move. They'll fall into the rhythm of the story and physically complement it.

Only the rarest story in the theater doesn't begin and end with some point of stillness, because everything has a beginning and an ending. Even in productions that skew the boundary at the beginning of a story by having actors interact with audience members from the moment they step into a theater, the play still has a beginning and ending, because a point of view regarding the play always exists for the actor and for the individual audience member. But plays that skew the boundaries are the exceptions. Before most every play begins, there's a moment of stillness, because stillness is, and always has been, the transition point between the end of one thing and the beginning of another. This makes a lot of sense, if considered, because in the beginning the earth was without form, and void, and darkness was upon the face of the deep. Then—light.

Be still whenever you can. This is the first, and most important, rule of movement. The more movement, the more distractions there are from the vocal instrument that is the center of all theatrical storytelling. All physical movement outside the vocal must be kept to a minimum, but, as with most every acting tool, a compromise must be found. A performance totally lacking in physical movement is as ineffective as a performance that utilizes constant physical movement. Physical movement is necessary to help support the effective building of tension and the establishment of rhythm.

The Effect of Style on Movement

Your first impulse concerning physical movement should always be to move only the parts of your body you need to move in order to communicate the text adequately. You should always look at every line and ask yourself, "Do I need to do more than simply stand (or sit or lean or whatever) here and simply deliver the text?" If you don't need to do more than that, then don't. If you do need to do more than that, then do *only what is necessary*. No more.

When considering how much and what kind of movement to utilize, first consider the style of the play. For our purposes, we'll define style as "the distinctive features characterizing a particular type of storytelling." Words commonly used to denote style are: drama, tragedy, comedy, tragicomedy (a mix of drama and comedy), melodrama, expressionism, and a host of others. Some styles are associated with certain individuals; for example, "Theater of Cruelty" is associated with Antonin Artaud and "Poor Theater" is associated with Jerzy Grotowski.

Considering style can be dangerous because, unless an actor is careful, keeping a style firmly in the forefront of the mind can lead to playing generalities. For instance, if you're constantly thinking of a play as being "comedic," it could lead you to utilizing a broad, extremely physical style of play and a loud, resonant voice even in those moments that don't require either. Considering style can be dangerous in the same way that considering states of being is dangerous, because neither puts you into action. You should think of style simply as a guide to the choices you make with the presentational tools. For instance, if you're playing a "comedic" character, such as the sprite Puck in *A Midsummer Night's Dream*, you'll most likely need to utilize a fairly broad and physical style of play. The performance of such a role will require you to use considerably more movement than playing a role such as Macbeth. Macbeth is a king, and any leader must give an impression of control. A sure and certain way to provide an impression of control is to be as still as possible.

An argument could be made that style has nothing whatsoever to do with these kinds of choices, and it would be a good argument. After all, Puck is a sprite, a sprite that likes to play tricks, and most of us probably are familiar with how sprites behave, particularly tricky ones, or at least are supposed to behave, physically speaking. We also know how rulers behave. In a sense, style is simply playing the obvious. While they're both characters in the same comedy, you could get into trouble approaching Theseus as someone similar to Puck. The difference, again, is in the obvious. Theseus is the Duke. Theseus is in control, or at the very least, believes he is, and acts upon his belief. Puck is a sprite that works for Oberon, and Oberon is a king, albeit king of the fairies. Theseus, being "king" of the mortals, probably doesn't move much. Shakespeare probably didn't intend for Theseus to move much. Puck moves. So does Oberon, as he is king of the fairies, but not like Puck moves. Oberon is a fairy *king*. Puck is all fairy.

Style can get you into trouble because, like emotion, it leads you into applying a generality to something that's specific. Generally speaking, the tempo of the beats in a comedy moves faster than the tempo of the beats in a drama, but this doesn't mean that everything in a comedy moves quickly and everything in a drama moves slowly. On the contrary, while it may be true that the tempo of comedy is faster than the tempo of drama, any play that's effective will contain moments that work best when the tempo moves quickly, moments that work best when the tempo moves slowly, and just about everything in between. Whether comedy or drama or some other style, each play should be approached with the same tools in mind.

Deciding When to Move

Style can be a general guideline for movement, but the *best* indicator of movement is the beat change. Some sort of movement always is necessary at the beginning of a beat. In fact, actors are forced to move at the beginnings of beats because most every beat begins with a line of dialogue. However, simply beginning to speak again, while an effective way of beginning a beat, is not the way most beats begin when theater is working. When theater is working, most beats begin with *physical movement* of some kind, and for a very good reason: In order to speak, you have to move in a physical way because you have to *take a breath*.

Using an example here may be helpful: In my workshop, actors sometimes present monologues while seated. They begin their monologues in stillness, relaxed and with their heads down. Before they deliver the first lines of their monologues, they raise their heads. In other words, they initiate the first beat by moving from a position of physical stillness. As they deliver the first beat of text, they use the presentational tools to build tension, and commonly, as they near the end of the first beat, they slow their tempo. As they reach the end of the beat, they cease movement—they "go still." Then, to initiate the second beat, they commonly *shift in their seats*. As with the beginning of the monologue, they move first, then begin to deliver the text. Not much time may pass between the initiation of the movement and the delivery of the text, but a little time must elapse because, in order to speak again, they must *take a breath*. Since, at the very least, an actor must take a breath, and thus move, to begin a beat, then in order to keep the delivery of the text as simple and uncluttered as possible, any extra-vocal (i.e., *physical*) movement should initiate at the beginning of the beat, on the breath.

This is exactly what happens when my students shift in their seats during their monologues, whether the shift comes at the beginning of the monologue or on a beat change: The physical shift begins on the inhalation. The physical movement may complete itself after delivery of the text has begun, but it almost always initiates on the breath. This "shift in the seat" can, of course, consist of myriad physical choices. An actor may start by sitting up straight, feet firmly on the floor, palms resting on his thighs. When he arrives at the first beat change, he goes still, if only for the briefest moment, then leans forward as he takes a breath, clasping his hands in front of him and resting his elbows on his thighs, and delivers the first line of the second beat. He could cross his legs and clasp his hands in his lap as he takes a breath, and then delivers the first line of the second beat. Depending on the limitations of the situation, he could, in fact, make any physical choice possible, including simply moving his head slightly as he takes a breath before he delivers the first line of the second beat. In any case, the pattern remains the same: physical movement—large or small—on the breath initiates the beat; vocal movement initiates almost immediately thereafter and continues throughout the beat; stillness occurs at the beat change; and physical movement initiates the second beat. This movement pattern is then repeated for *every* beat, until the end of the monologue, at which point the actor allows the stillness to hold, then puts his head down, relaxed and still, to indicate the end.

While it's possible to change a beat while seated without initiating some kind of extra-vocal movement, changing a beat in such a way is the vast exception to the rule. In order to change a beat strictly through vocalization, the moment of stillness—the caesura—between the end of one beat and the beginning of the next must be fairly long—a short pause rather than simply a beat or a hitch. Like every other acting tool discussed herein, while stillness works according to a set of rules, the rules are fluid and situational. If you are using physical movement to assist you in changing a beat, the stillness you utilize at the beat change that precedes the movement doesn't have to last long. A moment of stillness at a beat change is, however, always present in effective acting.

In addition, when a story in the theater is working, the actors are initiating almost all their larger physical movements on the beat changes. This is exactly what I described above—the "shifts in the seat" were the larger physical movements in the monologues. Almost without exception, larger physical movements occur strictly on beat changes. In other words, if an actor must cross from a chair on one side of the stage to a door on the other side of the stage, this large physical movement—the beginning of the cross—initiates at the beginning of a beat, most often as the actor takes a breath. Once movement is established, the movement can continue throughout the beat, as long as the cessation of movement occurs on the rhythm of the text. *All* physical movement should occur on the rhythm of the text. Establishing a strong sense of rhythm has everything to do with controlling the slow-fast-slow tempo structure of most beats and, when encountering a beat change, going still and initiating the next beat with some sort of physical movement on the breath. Moving to begin a beat is simply moving on the rhythm of the story.

Moving within a Beat

While you may feel secure in knowing that there is a sure indicator of larger physical movements, how can you know whether or not to move *within* a beat? For instance, if one actor is tasked to make a cross at the beginning of a beat, and the actor with the next line is tasked to follow the first actor, when should the second actor begin the physical movement and follow the first? The answer, I hope, is obvious: On the breath. The second actor begins to move—begins to follow the first—as he takes a breath to deliver his line. What if the second actor doesn't have a line, but is simply meant to follow as the other talks? Then the second actor should almost always begin to move on the punctuated rhythm of the speaker. In other words, the second actor begins to follow at a punctuated resting point (a comma, dash, period, etc.) in the speech of the other actor, and thus, on the rhythm of the text.

While this may sound unduly burdensome and technical, consider the alternative: random movement that works *against* the text rather than in support of it. You have only to observe how people in "real" life synchronize their words and movements to complement each other in order to understand why actors should do the same.

Textual Indications of Movement

The story you're telling may suggest some movement, and if movement is suggested, it's often in a parenthetical (the playwright is telling you to move in a parenthetical outside the scripted lines), or it's implied rather strongly within a line or lines of text. In both cases, you must *strongly consider* moving. Notice that I didn't say you should move or you have to move, but only that you should *strongly consider* moving. Often, the parentheticals in a script were written to address a specific set of circumstances, a set of circumstances that may have nothing whatsoever to do with the production in which you're a participant. Thus, the parentheticals may not be applicable to, or, for that matter, relevant to, what you're doing or being asked to do. You should give much more serious consideration to movement that's implied in the lines, as you may be undermining the story if something is implied and you're not doing it. This is particularly so for a tool I refer to as "focus"—a specialized and, like stillness, under-recognized and almost unacknowledged form of movement; the utilization of which the next chapter of this book outlines in detail. For instance Macbeth says, "Rather than so, come, fate, into the list." If he doesn't change his focal point as he says this line and "look at" fate, chances are the audience won't understand that he's speaking to a supernatural entity that isn't present on the stage.

Indication, Mugging, and Unconscious Movement

Even if a movement of some kind is implied in the lines, this doesn't give you license to indicate each and every thing a playwright may have written about. To be a bit more explicit, if a playwright has put a line in your mouth about "the earth, the trees, the air, and the sky," don't feel as if you must point to the earth and the trees, make a sweeping gesture to show you know where the air is, and point up in some fashion to the sky. Just because the playwright puts it in your mouth doesn't mean your hands, face, or body need to underline what comes out of it. This type of physical movement is commonly referred to as "indication" (i.e., you're "pointing out"—indicating—everything that's coming out of your mouth). A common form of indication is "mugging" (making faces), usually utilized to indicate an emotional state.

Often, actors will indicate without being aware of it, and this is a result of tension in the actor. If someone informs you that you're doing something physical and your immediate reaction is, "I didn't know I was doing that," this should tell you that you aren't in control of your instrument. An actor's instrument is his entire body and, as with a musical instrument, controlling it is possible, if one so desires. You control your instrument—it doesn't control you. However, you can allow it to control you, especially if you're constantly standing outside yourself and judging yourself. Unconscious physical movement is a sure indicator of an actor psychologically standing outside himself, and there are almost as many varieties of it as there are people who act. It could be constant eyebrow-bobbing, head-bobbing or head shaking, or "the clutchies" (hands clutched together in front at the waist); it could be finger rubbing, leg rubbing, or "claw-hand" (the hands tensed and claw-like, resting at the sides of the legs); it could be some form of tension placed in some part of the instrument, such as a stiff neck, an extended neck, stiff arms, or locked knees; it could be any or all of these things in combination. It could be "actor voice," a particularly common and loathsome form of unconscious physicality. If you have "actor voice," it means you speak in something other than your own voice while you're on the stage.

If you're moving onstage, or if you're placing tension somewhere in your instrument while onstage, and you aren't aware of it, you lack what I refer to as "self-knowledge." If you don't know what your "self"—i.e., your body, which is unarguably a part of your self—is doing at any given moment, at the very least, this unconscious physical movement indicates a lack of "self-awareness." I realize that this doesn't necessarily translate to a complete lack of self-knowledge, but if the two do not walk hand in hand, they at least march step for step.

Premodern audiences spoke of going to the theater to "hear" a play. (Take a look at the word "rehearsal"—see the "hear" in there?) The modern audience, like the premodern one, comes to the theater for the words and the story the words tell. (They actually come to see *people in action*—a big part of people in action, at least in the theater, is people *saying* things.) If you're constantly moving in an unconscious, habitual fashion or constantly placing tension in some part of your body in an unconscious, habitual fashion, you're not giving the audience the opportunity to concentrate on what they came for—the words. Psychologically speaking, the audience is wide open when they come to the theater, and they don't miss anything. While individual audience members may not consciously acknowledge the reasons something isn't working, on a subconscious level every audience member catches everything. Every audience is composed of expert viewers; we spend our lives telling and listening to stories, and as we are all born storytellers, so are we all born story listeners. You must choose the places you move in the same way you make choices about what's important in the text, and the movement choices you make must be based on the text. *Text-based choices* are the only ones you can count on. They are the only ones you can even justify.

Learning to Relax

If you constantly have things pointed out to you or find yourself doing things physically that you didn't intend to do, for at least fifteen minutes every day you should concentrate on *relaxing*. One effective relaxation exercise is to lie on the floor and release all the tension you find in your body. Start with your toes. Wiggle them around, feel the tension there, and release it. Then, move up your body, tensing and relaxing each major muscle group. Once you've worked your way up your body, lie there and concentrate on keeping your entire body relaxed. Once you've done this exercise a few times and have found it easier and easier to locate and release the tension in your body, change to a sitting position and do the same exercise. Repeat the same pattern and, when you're ready, go to a standing position and repeat the pattern again. Hopefully, as you move through the exercise, over time you'll discover where you're holding tension in your body.

I know this for certain: If you can't allow your instrument to relax in some form or fashion, you can't control it. If you're carrying unconscious tension in your body, whether through unconscious gesture or just through placing tension in some muscle group, you're not in control of your instrument—and you must control your instrument, the same way that a musician must, the same way that a dancer must. All your tools are contained in your instrument, and if you can't control your instrument, you can't control your tools, and you can't act effectively. If you can't learn how to control your instrument, to make it do exactly what you want and intend for it to do, then you'll have great difficulty becoming an effective actor. Of course, the most effective way of ensuring that you don't give your instrument over to unconscious movement or inadvertent tension is to have confidence in what you're presenting, and the surest way to gain such confidence, should you lack it, is to have a solid, simple, technique-oriented method of approaching text.

Gesture

Unless you're cast in a role that obviously calls for broad physicality, you can often limit the amount of movement you utilize within a beat. A tremendous number of actors are uncomfortable using their hands to gesture, and in most roles you need gesture very little in order to act effectively. While we all use our hands when we talk, at least to an extent, some of us use our hands very little, and it's perfectly acceptable for an actor to gesture very little. It is, in fact, to an actor's advantage to gesture as little as possible in order to support the story, because the primary focus should always be on the voice, and thus, on the text it delivers.

Some actors have the ability to gesture naturally and appropriately with their hands. This is an invaluable talent to possess because, next to actually getting over the hump of memorization, the inability to gesture naturally plagues a great many actors. Fortunately, the ability to gesture naturally onstage, like the ability to move well and gracefully, is overrated. If you use a gesture, it certainly should appear natural, but only in the rarest instances are you actually *required* to gesture with your hands.

Recently I was asked to evaluate the performance of a teenager in a high school production of Arthur Miller's *The Crucible*. She was playing a central role in the play, and when she was within a beat, for the most part her performance was effective. However, her overall performance was flat and affected, and the flatness and affectation were the result of two things: (1) She didn't appear to know what was important in the text, and thus, didn't change her tempo around the beat changes; and (2) Most of her gestures were stiff and self-conscious. Like most actors, she had difficulty gesturing with her hands. The suggestions I made to the director were: (1) Get her to slow her tempo when delivering important material around the beat changes; and (2) Have her use only those gestures with which she appeared comfortable.

I had the opportunity to see this young lady perform the role again, and the effect of making these simple changes was astounding. While she didn't give a great performance, she gave an adequate one, and there's much to be said for adequacy. Most astounding was the fact that she gestured with her hands barely a half-dozen times, and all were effective. The majority of the time, her hands rested at her sides. In other words, she basically *stopped* gesturing for the length of her performance, and it didn't hurt her performance one bit. On the contrary, it helped.

Keep in mind that movement and the effect it has are always proportional to the amount of overall movement at any given moment in a scene. In other words, like all the presentational tools, *movement is relative*. However, the relative effect of the presentational tools is even more pronounced with movement because giving voice to the text provides constant movement. Thus, any other physical movement has the potential of distracting from the text.

An example may be helpful here also: If, in a scene, you're standing and talking with another character onstage and neither one of you is utilizing any other kind of physical movement, chances are the first physical movement one of you makes is going to read to the audience as very, very big, even if it is only a tiny, tiny movement. This is so because neither one of you has been physically moving. However, if two actors are physically moving around on the stage constantly throughout the course of the scene, none of the movement really has any impact, because the actors have been moving so much; therefore, no single movement carries any weight. (What would carry weight in a situation like this? The *cessation* of movement.)

Consider this particularly in terms of gesture. Let's say you're standing alone on a stage delivering a monologue, and you're standing up straight with your hands relaxed at your sides. The first time you bring your arm or arms up to gesture, it's going to mean a lot because of the still position that you start from. And the larger the gesture gets, the bigger it's going to read. (The same can be said of tempo: If you're driving the tempo very quickly and then slow down for a phrase, the more you slow down, the more important the phrase is going to read.) So, if you want something you're saying to read as being perhaps even more important than it otherwise would be, raise a hand and gesture outside the range of (i.e., away from) your body. If, however, you simply want to emphasize something you're saying, raise a hand and keep it within the range of (i.e., close to) your body. In either case, you're going to draw attention to whatever it is you're saying, either in a big way or a small way. With any gesture, when you're finished with it, let that hand or those hands come to rest again at your sides. *Relaxed.* Don't leave them hanging up there unless you want to somehow hold whatever tension you've created. Whatever you do, do it on purpose, with thought and consideration behind it.

If you decide a gesture is necessary early in a beat, don't just bring a hand up, use it for a brief moment, and then release it for the remainder of the beat. If you believe a gesture is necessary early in a beat, once you've raised a hand and started to use it, keep it there and use it for the entire beat.

While we are once again treading on dangerous ground here, I will be as specific as I can. Human beings, generally speaking, don't just gesture once and then never gesture again. If a person begins to gesture, the gesture will remain present until that person has made her point, and then the gesture will release. In the theater, if you introduce a gesture, it should remain present throughout any given beat, and then, as described above, hold at the beat change and release as the next beat begins. In addition, you may introduce a gesture early in a beat and then drop it, but only if you then bring it up again within a phrase or within a few words of its first use. In other words, you may gesture and release it; then gesture again and release it; and then gesture again, all within a single beat—as long as the gesture, while it may not always be present, comes and goes and comes and goes, until finally, toward the end of the beat, it remains present, holds at the beat change, and then releases.

You could make an argument that, in such a case, an actor would be constantly moving, as the gesture would constantly be present. But if I bring a finger up and point at you, then just simply hold the finger there until I want to emphasize something else I'm saying, then jab it at you at the point of emphasis, then hold it up there, motionless, until I want to emphasize something else, and then repeat the pattern, I'd argue that the only time I'm actually moving is when I'm jabbing the finger. If, on the other hand, I bring the finger up and just keep jabbing it and jabbing it, then everything weighs the same and all the movement means nothing.

Finally, be extremely careful about using a repetitive gesture for any great length of time. If you use the same gesture over and over again during a beat, or during successive beats, the audience will be distracted by the gesture, because gesturing in such a way is unnatural. If you introduce a gesture within a beat, always try to vary it at least once in at least some small way. In life, people almost never use the same gesture over and over again (unless, of course, they're politicians, most of whom could use some effective acting training). Rather, they may use the same gesture for a short period of time, and then vary it either within, or very near the end of, a point they're making.

Writing about gesture is, to say the least, difficult without a practical visual demonstration, so try this: Watch people as they're talking, and start paying attention to the way they use their hands. You'll find that what I've written above holds true over a wide range of people and situations. In fact, you'll find that the only situation where you'll see people gesturing in a consistently repetitive and unnatural way is when, like politicians and actors, they're speaking in public.

Listening and Stillness

The rules that apply to movement also apply to listening. When we listen in life, we almost never move. If we do move, the movement is usually very small and matches the speaker's rhythm. In other words, we complement the speaker when we listen. If you think about it, this makes perfect sense: Anything we do in life, including listening, is directed at the person who's with us. All our physical, vocal, and mental actions are directed at *other people*, so any movement we make while listening should be directed at the person to whom we're listening, in order to have some kind of effect on that person.

Moving your body or, more commonly, your face, in a constant manner while listening onstage just doesn't make sense. We rarely do such a thing in life, so why do so many people do it so often onstage? If you're constantly moving your face or body while listening onstage, what you're really doing is *indicating* that you're listening, *illustrating* that you're listening. Most actors never actually listen when they're onstage except for their next cue, so they can say their next line. They don't listen as they do in life. *In life, listening is interactive.* You listen in order to interact with the person who's speaking. You listen to have an effect on the speaker. In a sense, you listen "for" that other person, to let that other person know you're paying attention. You allow that other person to move while you cease movement—or, at the very least, lessen movement considerably. You allow that other person to control your attention. If you do move, it's to complement the speaker, to work with the speaker, to work on the speaker, to let the speaker know that the speaker is in control and you're doing nothing more or less than following along.

On the stage, on the other hand, for many actors—and I'm talking about the way things *are* now, not the way things *should be*—listening is *reactive*. You do it for yourself, to draw attention to yourself. "See me?" you say to that audience, "I'm listening now." You stand outside yourself mentally and act for the audience rather than for the person onstage with you. Some actors, when listening, stop "acting" altogether. They become *non*-active. Not only do they not speak or not listen, but they don't even *indicate* that they're listening. Their faces and bodies go dead until it's their turn to speak again. (This "deadness" sometimes happens with actors who are attempting to "go still" at beat changes; rather than simply ceasing to move, they "go dead," and all the energy drains from their bodies and faces. With such actors, it's often helpful to tell them to think of the stillness as a "freeze." They "freeze" for a moment at the beat change, and then move as they begin the next beat. This often seems to take the "deadness" out of their "stillness.")

Listening onstage should be just like listening in life. Interactive, not reactive or non-active. We get ourselves into trouble because we try to make the theater something other than life. It isn't. It's life. *Real* life. Flesh and blood and bone and marrow, mind and body moving through time and space.

The Rules of Movement

Below are the rules of movement. One of these rules refers to "focus," which I haven't detailed yet; that's coming along real soon:

1. First, be still. Then—
2. Move if it's going to support the story you're telling. This means—
   a. Relatively larger physical movements will be initiated on the beat changes.

b. Focus changes will be utilized in accordance with the text.

c. Gestures will be utilized minimally, selectively, and relative to overall need.

3. But always—

a. Move only if you have to, and—

b. Move only if it's a conscious choice.

The Ability to Move Freely

Certainly it's possible for an actor who has a talent for movement to simply allow his instrument to move freely. When human beings speak, often their heads will move in rhythm with their speech. Often, a person will use one hand, or both, to accent or underline his speech in a rhythmic way. Be careful, though. Unless you know—unless you're absolutely certain—that you possess the ability to move your instrument freely, don't even attempt it. Instead, choose every movement you make in a conscious, text-based fashion.

If you do possess the ability to move freely and naturally, then you can use that ability in chosen beats. In other words, because you don't ever want to weigh the text down with movement, in most beats you'll be still, relatively speaking. However, you may find beats in which you wish to accent the rhythm of your text, and thus, build tension by adding a gesture with your head or hands and allowing that gesture, like the jabbing finger, to live in the beat—to accent the rhythm, and even the build of the tempo, as you speak.

Should you decide to use this type of gesture, keep in mind that it eventually needs to *release*. This is particularly so with hand gestures. Once you've finished gesturing in a beat such as the one described immediately above, at the end of the beat the gesture should hold on the stillness, then release on the breath as the next beat begins. This release can then serve as the movement that begins the next beat. In other words, if you have raised a hand and used it to "keep time" with the rhythm of your text, then when you reach the beat change, the gesture will hold with the stillness, then release as or before the next breath is taken and the next beat begins. This "release" will most likely consist of dropping your hands to your sides if you're standing, or letting them come to rest in or near your lap in some way if you're sitting. In any case, the gesture should release, and thus, allow the tension in the audience to release as well. This is, in fact, exactly what happens when beat changes are working effectively: After the moment of stillness in which the tension holds, the actor releases the tension by moving at the beginning of the next beat.

If you have the ability to move naturally and freely, you have a valuable talent. But don't use such ability arbitrarily, because eventually, everything will weigh the same, and if everything weighs the same, your storytelling will lack the tension on which it thrives.

CHAPTER 15

Focus

"FOCUS" IS WHERE YOU LOOK WHEN YOU'RE ONSTAGE. Like so many of the actor's tools, focus operates according to a set of rules, but unlike most of the "rules" we've been discussing— which, for the most part, are not hard-and-fast rules—the rules of focus are practically written in stone.

The Rules of Focus

The rules of focus that I'm about to detail may sound somewhat irreverent. The irreverent tone is purposeful, and I'll explain that shortly. The rules of focus are:

- Focus on the person who's speaking or who's listening to you speak (your primary focal point)
- *Never* remove your focus from a person who's speaking
- Besides focusing on the person who's speaking or who's listening to you speak, there are only three other things (secondary focal points) you should focus on:
  - An animate or inanimate object, or set of objects, whether present onstage or not
  - Something you are or another person is doing
  - For lack of a better term, "inwardly."
- *Never* focus on nothing (i.e., "empty space")

So, why the irreverent tone? If you're speaking onstage, focus on the person (or persons, if there are more than one, "splitting" your focus in such a case) who's listening to you speak, and if you're not speaking, focus on the person who is.

That should always be your *primary focal point*—the person or persons who are listening to you speak or who are speaking to you. And while it may seem obvious, when I say to focus on them, I mean look *at their eyes*. Your *secondary focal point*, if there is one, will be one of the three things just mentioned: an animate or inanimate object, or set of objects, whether present onstage or not; something you are or another person is doing; or inwardly.

That fourth rule about never focusing on nothing may seem a bit confusing, but I see actors focusing on nothing all the time, i.e., letting their focus *bounce*. Often you'll see actors whose eyes constantly move from spot to spot, and, like any repetitive movement, through sheer volume, none of it means anything at all. It's not that you can never "bounce" your focus, but if you're going to do so, a sound, text-based reason for it must exist.

I didn't really mean the "nevers" I put in those rules. I stuck those "nevers" in there so that you would understand that focusing on the speaker/listener is of *paramount* importance in the theater. While you may believe that there are many instances in which a character isn't supposed to be looking at another character who's speaking, I'd disagree. In the theater, situations in which you aren't required to look at a speaker are the vast exception to the rule, because the words of the play are almost invariably the center of what's happening, and bouncing your focus in the manner described above does nothing but detract from the words of the play.

The Importance of Focus

Focus is so important in the theater because it tells the audience what's important. In movies and television, a camera tells us where to focus. It tells us exactly what's important, and it tells us all of the time. It follows the focal point of any given scene wherever that focal point happens to go. Whether it's to a person, a hand, an animal, whatever and however, that camera follows it and tells us, "See? That's what's important. Look at it." You have little choice (except to look away from the screen).

No cameras in the theater. No omniscient point of view telling us where to look. We can choose to look at anything we wish, but if, at any given point in a play, an actor looks somewhere other than where is necessary in order for the audience to understand the story, the audience will have difficulty following what's happening. The audience needs to be allowed to see and hear what's important in the theater in the same way that it needs to be allowed to see and hear what's important in a film, but with this difference: In the theater the audience's focus is manipulated by the way the actors onstage manipulate their focus. The actors tell the audience what's important in the story; they clue the audience in on how they should observe and, ultimately, on how to receive the story.

Focus as Movement

Focus is a form of movement because when you change your focus—look from one thing to another—you move. Sometimes you move just your eyes, sometimes your head, sometimes your whole body, but in each case, you're moving. Therefore, like any other type of physical movement, moving to change your focus is secondary in importance to the primary movement of the vocal instrument, and its use should be limited strictly to choices gleaned from the text.

Because stillness should be an actor's physical base, as with any other type of movement, you need to find those moments in the text where changing your focus will support the story. In the vast majority of scenes, only two focal points will be found: a *primary* focal point and *secondary* focal points. The primary focal point will usually, though not always, be the speaker/listener. Of course, the primary focal point can change every time a different character speaks, but the nature of the focal point remains the same: the speaker/listener. Like primary focal points, secondary focal points can also change. For example, the primary focal point for Marnie in the scene from *Perdita* in appendix C is Goldie. Secondary focal points include the curtains, the pill bottles, the neighbors, and the memories of which she speaks.

Focusing "inwardly" (i.e., on "nothing") is a type of secondary focal point that should be used sparingly. Commonly, when you observe a person trying to recall something, she looks upward, as if looking into her own head, or downward. (You need to be very careful about looking downward onstage, because chances are you'll be hiding your face from the audience, so you'd better be enunciating well since the audience won't be able to see your mouth). While an argument could be made that, if a character is remembering something during a play and shifts her focus off the listener, the character is then focusing on nothing, I would counter that the character isn't focusing on nothing, but rather on the memory of which she speaks. The character is, in a sense, focusing "inwardly." When focus is thought of in this way, I think it becomes very difficult to focus on nothing, because if you're focusing on nothing, you must be asleep, dead, or simply not a very effective actor.

Choosing When and Where to Focus

Below is a score for Portia from Shakespeare's *The Merchant of Venice*. (As always, note the form of the score: beats marked with slashes; key phrases bolded rather than circled; and key words underlined.)

> **The quality of mercy is not <u>strain'd</u>;**
> It droppeth as the gentle rain from <u>heaven</u>
> Upon the place beneath. **It is <u>twice</u> blest;**
> It blesseth him that <u>gives</u> and him that <u>takes</u>./
> **'Tis mightiest in the <u>mightiest</u>:** it becomes
> The throned monarch <u>better</u> than his crown;
> **His scepter shows the force of <u>temporal</u> power,**
> The <u>attribute</u> to awe and majesty,
> Wherein doth sit the dread and <u>fear</u> of kings./
> **But mercy is <u>above</u> this sceptr'd sway.**
> It is enthroned in the <u>hearts</u> of kings.
> It is an attribute to **God himself.**
> And <u>earthly</u> power doth then show <u>likest</u> God's
> **When mercy seasons justice.**

What's the primary focal point in this piece of text? When performing a familiar piece of text—every director out there knows *The Merchant of Venice* (and if he doesn't, he probably shouldn't be directing)—you must be familiar with the context. In this speech, Portia is pretending to be a young male lawyer in an attempt to persuade Shylock to show mercy to Antonio, who agreed to surrender a pound of flesh if he did not repay a debt. While you could get hung up on the "male" part of those circumstances, that's actually the least important part. (If everyone on the stage accepts that Portia is a young man, and the designers have seen fit to costume Portia as a young man, then everyone will accept that Portia is a young man, whether or not the actor performing the role acts and sounds like a young man.)

This is powerful material and a well-reasoned argument. Any actor delivering this monologue need do no more than the physical minimum: stand up straight with her hands relaxed at her sides. Portia is replying directly to a comment of Shylock's when this speech begins. This means that Portia's primary focal point is Shylock, and so she'll look directly at Shylock for the majority of the text.

What if the actor were presenting this piece as a monologue for an audition, and no actor playing Shylock was present? In that case, the primary focal point would be a point in space somewhere toward the center of the theater, but never on the person or persons for whom she is auditioning. When auditioning, never look at the person or persons for whom you're auditioning. They may have other things to do, and your looking at them will force a commitment on their part to return your gaze. Rather, choose a focal point that's obviously above their heads if you're on a higher level than them, or to the left or right. In either case, choose a point that's in front of you, as Shylock would most likely be standing in front of you as you speak to him, and choose a point as close to the center of the theater as possible, so as to allow the person or persons for whom you're auditioning to see as much of your instrument as possible.

Are there secondary focal points in the monologue? Take a good hard look at it. Really break the language down. What's it about? It's about *mercy*, yes? Every line of the verse, except for three of them, is directed at the idea of mercy (and a strong argument could be made that even those three exceptional lines are directed at the idea of mercy). Every beat is about mercy: The first beat is about the quality of mercy; the second about mercy in the monarch; the third about how the monarch becomes god-like by showing mercy. Is there a way to show "mercy" onstage? According to the monologue, mercy is an attribute of God, and God or heaven is referred to no fewer than three times.

You can make mercy palpable on the stage by using God as a secondary focal point. I'd go so far as to suggest that the movement in the speech can be limited to exactly the following: (1) delivering the text; (2) using Shylock as the primary focal point and God as the secondary focal point; and (3) slight physical movement to help change the beats.

For instance, stand up straight and relaxed, with your hands at your sides, and put your head down. You're now in position to begin the monologue. Since the primary focal point of the monologue is Shylock, raise your head and look at a point across from you, as if you're speaking to someone right in front of you. That point in front of you, for this monologue, is Shylock. After you raise your head, let the stillness hold for a brief moment and then deliver this entire speech to the primary focal point, with one exception. As you say the word "heaven," look up, as if looking at the sky above you, letting your focus hold briefly at the height of the movement, and hitch (stop delivering the text for a brief moment—this will help key the word "heaven," which has been underlined). Then, as you begin delivering the next part of the text, let your head slowly return to its original position so that your focus is again placed on Shylock as you say the word "beneath."

Next to moving on the beat changes, that is the only extra-vocal movement this piece requires. No hand gestures. No moving of the feet or arms. Just an actor, standing up straight and shifting her focus once. As for the movement on the beat changes, one need only go still at the end of the previous beat and, on the breath for the next beat, move the head slightly—for instance, raising the chin just a bit as the breath is taken—never removing the focus from Shylock. Then, let it rest in its original position as the next beat of text is delivered. Keep in mind that "going still" (ceasing movement) at the beat changes is of paramount importance, because little in the way of physical movement is being used to change the beats. If the slight physical movements are to read, and thus assist in changing the beats, the movements must come from a point of stillness.

There certainly are moments in this monologue where a hand gesture or other movement outside of what I've suggested could be used appropriately. I'm not saying additional hand gestures or other movements are not appropriate here. I'm simply saying they're not *required*, that an actor with a loud, clear voice and a well-considered score, one who is willing to commit to the choices outlined above, can effectively deliver this particular monologue. Will it be great acting? No way to tell, but again, great acting is not what we're looking for; competency, and thus, adequacy, are.

I'm not sure I can overemphasize the importance of this tool. Focus—where to focus and why—should fall very high on any actor's list of priorities. When directing, I discuss focus with actors before I discuss action. My first working rehearsal with a group of actors centers on discussing the focal points in a scene and how to manipulate them to help tell the story.

A Further Example of Manipulating Focus

Before we leave the subject of focus, take another look at the Macbeth monologue in appendix B. How many focal points are there in this speech?

Since it's a soliloquy, there's the audience. I know that there are directors of Shakespeare's plays—and other plays, for that matter—who would never dream of having an actor speak directly to the audience while delivering a soliloquy. I think that's really inconsiderate, and worse, that it completely ignores one of the most special things about live theater: the ability of the living to contact the living.

Whenever you encounter a chance to focus on the audience, you should focus on the audience. You know the audience is there, they know you're there, and they know you know they're there. If you encounter an opportunity to focus on them and don't, what does that say to them? That you're "pretending" they aren't there? (And who among them is going to believe that?) That you don't care about them? That they aren't really necessary to the story? If focusing on the audience isn't going to violate the story and the audience isn't going to feel threatened by the focus, then focus on them. If the audience might feel threatened, then be very careful about focusing on them—but in most cases, an audience won't feel threatened by an actor focusing on them. Almost without exception, an audience will welcome the contact. In the case of the *Macbeth* soliloquy, the audience certainly won't feel threatened. At least, they certainly didn't during the one production of the play I directed, because during each of his soliloquies and asides, Macbeth focused on the audience throughout the course of the performance. In that particular production, the audience was split into two very distinct halves, so in order to speak to all of them, Macbeth had to focus on both sides, thus giving him a split primary focal point.

What about secondary focal points? Banquo certainly is one, since the soliloquy is about him. In the production referred to above, there was an entrance/exit point downcenter, directly between the two halves of the audience. The actor playing Banquo exited there just before Macbeth delivered this soliloquy, so Macbeth used that entrance/exit as his focal point for Banquo. One could argue that, by focusing in this way, Macbeth was focusing on "nothing," but he actually was focusing on Banquo. That entrance/exit point downcenter, in a sense, *became* Banquo, because Macbeth placed his focus there so often when talking about Banquo. In other words, in the same way that "mercy" was made present onstage by the use of focus in the Portia speech, Banquo remained "present" onstage because Macbeth kept him there by establishing that secondary focal point.

Any other secondary focal points? Perhaps at the end, but I'll get to that. Otherwise, that's really all you need for the majority of this soliloquy: *two focal points,* the primary focal point being the two halves of the audience and the secondary focal point being Banquo.

How to manipulate the focal points? In the production I've been describing, the initial connection with the audience was established by Macbeth delivering the first phrase ("To be thus is nothing") to one side of the audience and the second phrase ("But to be safely thus") to the other side. This established contact with both sides of the audience, making them equals. The next two and a half lines, beginning with "Our fears in Banquo stick deep," were delivered to the Banquo focal point. Then, Macbeth turned his focus to one side of the audience for "'Tis much he dares," and to the other side for the next two and a half lines. Then, back to the Banquo focal point for "There is none but he/Whose being I do fear, and under him/My genius is rebuked, as it is said/Marc Antony's was by Caesar."

In the next beat, from "He chid the sisters" through "No son of mine succeeding," Macbeth's focus was again split between the two halves of the audience, matching the rhythm of the focus changes with the rhythm of the lines. In other words, Macbeth delivered the "He chid the sisters" sentence to one side, and the "Then prophet-like" sentence to the other side. He then split up the next four lines, two to one side, then two to the other. This last helped build the tempo, and thus the tension, for focusing downcenter toward the Banquo focal point for the "If 't be so" section of lines.

The end of the speech is tricky. The "eternal jewel" is most likely Macbeth's soul and that's a difficult focal point to establish. Since the end of the soliloquy was near, the actor playing Macbeth did something that helped build toward the last sentence of the speech. To begin with, he focused up (toward heaven) for the "eternal jewel" phrase, down for "the common enemy of man" phrase (the common enemy of man being the devil), back to the Banquo focal point for "to make them kings," etc., then back up, into the air, for the final sentence, "fate," in a sense, being "God."

Context Is Everything

This focal analysis of Macbeth's soliloquy was done with a certain set of themes in mind, all of which were gleaned from the text, and a certain spacial configuration that was in place.

What if you want to use this monologue as an audition piece and need to deliver it in a proscenium theater? The focal points don't change, but where you place them may. Most proscenium theaters have a raised stage, with the first row of the audience down toward the actor's feet and the rest of the rows rising up and away toward the back of the house. Split the auditorium in two, using the two halves as the primary focal point, and place Banquo straight in front of you, up at the back of the house. The "eternal jewel" and "common enemy of man" focal points remain the same. Once an actor has analyzed a piece for focal points, he should be able to adjust those focal points no matter what space he's asked to perform in, because the focal points don't change—only the placement of them does, and in most instances, even this won't change significantly.

Any piece of text can be analyzed for focal points by identifying the primary focal point, identifying every possible secondary focal point (of which only a limited number, usually a very limited number, will exist), and deciding which focal point you need to give your focus to at any given point in a scene in order to tell the story effectively. Once you're certain you have identified the focal points, *use only those focal points you have identified.* Don't get distracted. Don't ever imagine that somehow the rules of focus will bend to the breaking point just for you. The rules of focus bend, but not much. Don't allow yourself to be self-centered. Center on exactly what's important: the story you tell and the work that you do.

CHAPTER 16

Beat Actions

WE CAN'T HELP BUT PUT OURSELVES INTO ACTION. In life, whenever we're awake, and often when we aren't, we're in action, working on others for certain ends. Any actor that walks onto a stage is putting himself into action. Most actors I've seen seem to be playing precisely the same action all of the time: to please the audience. Without question, this is an action. "To please" is an effective transitive verb that implies a strong set of physical and vocal tactics and, when used in the way I'm describing, it's directed at a human object. "To please the audience" works in exactly the way an effective action statement should work, but chances are the vast majority of the time, if not 100 percent of the time, this action will do nothing to assist an actor in effectively presenting a text, because the actor isn't working within the story.

An argument could be made that "to please the audience" is the ultimate aim of any piece of theater, or any other art form for that matter. I admit there's truth in that, but there's also a problem with it. The actor is at the center of the art form known as theater, and if the idea behind any art form is "to please the audience," it's a short step for *an actor* to believe that he must please the audience, all on his own, or the theater will fail. This isn't the case at all. If audiences attended the theater only to see brilliant actors, community and regional theater wouldn't flourish in this country, as it always has and always will. If people were interested only in seeing the Daniel Day-Lewises and Meryl Streeps of this world, then the only theater that would flourish would be the professional theater. People come to the theater not to see brilliant acting, although I'm certain audiences will take it if they can get it. People come to the theater to see a good story well told, and all good stories in the theater involve *people in action*.

Utilizing Beat Actions

Beat actions are an analytical tool, but I include them under "Presentation" because they dictate the use of the presentational tools. Any effective transitive verb will imply a strong set of physical and vocal tactics that can be directed at a human object, and this is exactly what you seek when writing an action statement, whether it is a main action or beat actions. The main action is what an actor needs to concentrate on in performance; it assists the actor in activating his performance. While an actor may also find it useful to focus on specific beat actions during a performance, I suggest that beat actions primarily be used during the rehearsal process to assist in choices concerning physical and vocal tactics.

Consider the beat actions for the *Macbeth* monologue in appendix B. Below are the definitions for each of the verbs:

- Intrigue: to arouse the interest or curiosity of
- Alert: to notify of approaching danger or action; warn
- Ignite: to set on fire
- Impassion: to arouse the passions of
- Invoke: to summon with incantations; conjure

If you accept that a monologue is a little scene, then it follows that any monologue will reflect, in some way, the four-part pattern of storytelling—exposition/building action/climax/denouement. This is exactly the pattern you'll find if you examine the *Macbeth* monologue. It is also exactly the pattern you'll find if you examine the beat actions chosen for the monologue. If the aim of any given play, act, scene, or beat is to build tension, then the beat actions will reflect, to some extent if not to a great extent, the building of tension if well chosen, and this is exactly what you find in the beat actions outlined above.

"Intrigue" means "to arouse," and certainly "arousing" someone is very different from "warning" him. One of the definitions of "alert" is "to warn," and in this way you can see how the second beat builds on and heightens any tension created in the first. "Ignite" means "to set on fire," and again this action builds on the previous one and further builds the tension. "Setting something on fire" is, again, different from "arousing the passions of"—if you set something on fire, it doesn't immediately become a conflagration, but if you arouse the passions of someone, those passions will burn intensely very quickly.

Through effectively using these four verbs—intrigue, alert, ignite, impassion—it is, I believe, easy to see how an actor can work this piece of text to build tension. In addition, because each of these actions—with the exception of "intrigue"—indicates a necessary change of vocal tactics, one beat to the next, the actions dictate a build within the monologue. Either through the use of tempo, volume, or intensity, the vocal tension builds through each successive beat and climaxes on "to make them kings, the seeds of Banquo kings," which is the highest point in the monologue (and should therefore receive the most sustained volume and/or intensity).

As for "invoke," it is very different from the other four actions chosen. It comes in the beat that is the denouement of the monologue, and therefore implies a very different vocal choice than the other actions. The choices it would be most similar to are the choices made for the first beat—"intrigue"—but, as with any denouement, "invoke" implies a slightly different, quicker tempo choice than "intrigue," and this is usually the case for the denouement of a beat (or scene, or act, or play). The denouement, while having a slower tempo than the building action and the climax, will have a slightly quicker tempo than the exposition. In addition, because "invoke" means "to summon with incantations," it implies a use of resonance that's very different from the other chosen actions.

None of which is to say a climax cannot come in a quiet way. It can, but quiet climaxes are the exception to the rule. Climaxes are the highest moments in any story, and it's quite possible that a climax can be "built down" to as well as "built up" to. But climaxes that build down are rare. The climax of almost every play—and act, scene, set of beats, or beat—will come toward the end and, in almost every instance, receive more than its fair share of tempo, volume, and/or intensity.

If you're working logically and effectively, for any given monologue you'll always be able to find a set of beat actions like the one outlined above. The same can be said, to a certain extent, of scenes. If you examine the scene score in appendix C, you'll see that the beat actions outlined for the character Marnie ebb and flow during the course of the scene. For instance, the first four beat actions—embrace, corner, occupy, encourage—build in a similar way to the actions outlined for the *Macbeth* monologue. "Embrace" is exceptional, in a way, as Marnie enters with one intention, which is dashed immediately by Goldie. Thus, Marnie adjusts her action, with "occupy" building on "corner" and "encourage" building on "occupy." If you examine the lines in conjunction with the chosen actions for the first four beats of the scene, then, in combination, the actions make up the first part of the larger story of the scene, as the last three beats are about the neighbors and what they're up to.

Given this kind of pattern, it's tempting to postulate yet another acting tool. As we have plays, plays have acts, and acts have scenes that are divided into beats, and as beats seem to group themselves around even larger ideas, just as they do in the *Perdita* scene score, postulating the idea of another kind of scene—a demi-scene, if you will—isn't out of the question. However, if you're writing your beat actions effectively and, more importantly, using them to dictate your choices concerning the uses of the presentational tools, dividing scenes into anything smaller or larger than a beat is not necessary. The effective utilization of the beat actions will do that for you.

It's also certainly possible to write beat actions to reflect other kinds of patterns within a story. For instance, for a beat that builds down, the first beat action would most likely imply a use of volume very different from the beat action at the end of a scene. As an example, a character might enter a room intending to damn another character, and end up forgiving that character at the end of the scene. Chances are the beat actions for this particular character would build down during the scene, from "to damn" to "to forgive." Another interesting pattern of beat actions would be necessary for a character that is meant to build up and then knock down another character repeatedly over the course of a monologue; e.g., "to assure," "to incite," "to cajole," and "to impel."

The Importance of Beat Actions

Are beat actions really necessary? Couldn't you decide, for instance, what kind of tempo or volume or focus you need in any given beat without writing an action for the beat? An example, I believe, might be helpful here.

"Flatter" is an effective action verb, as it implies a strong set of physical and vocal tactics; e.g., you're most likely going to smile at the object of the flattery and you're most likely going to use a loud, clear, even voice. What if the flattery is returned in kind? You might then decide to "flirt." "Flirt" is similar to "flatter," but if you're "flirting," then chances are you'll speak in a louder voice, you'll use a quicker overall tempo, and your focus will bounce toward and away from the object of your flirtation, almost as if you're fly-fishing. (This example is also instructive because the verb "flirt" is intransitive. While one can force it to take a human object by adding the word "with," and thus "make" it transitive, on its own it merely implies a physical quality. However, without question, "flirt" is playable, especially when combined with the word "with.") If the flirting is returned in kind, you might then decide to "arouse" the object of the flattery. "Arouse," while it certainly builds on the pattern that has been established with "flatter" and "flirt," implies a significant change in physical and vocal tactics. The voice is no longer so loud and the overall tempo is no longer so quick. The focus stops bouncing and lands squarely on the object of arousal, never wavering, and chances are excellent that you move physically closer. "Seduce" is similar to "arouse," but different; if you choose to seduce someone, chances are you're fairly certain of success, and body-to-body contact is now very much in the equation. If there's body-to-body contact in arousal, it's probably leg-to-leg or arm-to-arm, and in flirtation, there's probably no body-to-body contact at all, unless it's a light touch on the arm or shoulder.

Now, you could probably decide to do any or all of these things without writing beat actions. And some of those choices you make might be due to a close reading of the script and your intuition regarding what's happening. But why rely on "intuition," a non-rational process, when you actually can examine the text and, at the very least, attempt to deduce what's actually happening? Why determine something by impulse when you can determine it by reason?

Focus Your Mind

If you're an actor, your art is in words, and this is particularly so for writing actions. Becoming familiar with words and the intricacies and implications of their meanings is paramount to your effective use of the presentational tools. In rehearsal, either on your own or with others, you can use your beat actions to assist you in making choices concerning all of the presentational tools, because the actions you choose, if you choose them effectively, will imply strong sets of physical and vocal tactics that allow the story to ebb and flow. Whenever you're in doubt about a physical or vocal choice, considering the beat action you've gleaned from the text will assist you in making the most effective presentational choices possible.

Most importantly, having and utilizing an effective set of beat actions will keep your mind focused squarely on the stage throughout any rehearsal process and, in the end, during performance as well. Unless you are in a one-person show or presenting a monologue in which you speak directly to the audience, your action should never be directed at the audience, and for very good reason: Your head will be out there instead of on the stage, in the story, where it belongs. In a sense, the audience completes the actor; after all, without an audience, no theater can exist. The audience is an essential component of the theatrical process. All art, no matter what form it takes, is a social exercise, for without a group of people, no art form is possible. Of course, we want to please the audience, but our ability to please the audience comes not through our desire to do so; rather, it comes through our ability to tell a story in the most effective manner possible.

PART 3

Activation

CHAPTER 17

Plan and Process

BREAKING A PLAY DOWN INTO ITS COMPONENT PARTS is easy if you accept that storytelling is formulaic. A script is inert and invites a breaking down. But even this breaking down will only take us so far, since the actual process of delivering the text is *a living thing*. There's nothing inert about it. While it serves our purposes to break the text, and even the delivery of text, into parts, into tools, in an ultimate sense the tools have to come back together to make a whole because *the delivery of text is alive*. In an ultimate sense, acting resists being broken down. And like any living thing, if you break it down too far, you kill it.

More than one person has told me that I make acting sound easy. Given what you've read thus far in this book, you may have difficulty believing that, but it's true. I don't mean to make it sound easy, but I do think that understanding the basic tools of acting *is* easy. There just aren't that many of them, the same way that a painter who uses watercolor ultimately doesn't have that many tools to deal with. But it's not about the tools. It's about what you do with the tools. Sure, there are a limited number of colors in the spectrum, but when you actually start to mix them—watch out.

If you wish to act effectively, you first must accept who you are. If you're small and heavy, chances are you'll never play a lover (or, if you do, you will be a very special kind of lover). If you're a woman, chances are you'll never play King Lear. Look in the mirror, know yourself, and accept.

If you wish to act effectively, you also must have a mind within the range of normal, a loud, clear voice, and an understanding of all the actor's tools—particularly a thorough understanding of the beat, the most important tool in analysis, and of tempo, the most important tool in presentation. Focusing on clear analysis and clean presentation will go a long way toward allowing you to reach your potential as an actor. There is, however, a final step in the acting process, without which acting remains little more than an academic exercise. If you're to act effectively in the truest sense, you also must *activate* your performance—allow it to *live*.

There's a book about acting, now seemingly out of print, called *Acting is Doing*. I've always had trouble with that title. It implies something that can only serve to divert the focus of any actor, because acting isn't just doing, it's doing *with a purpose*. That's why I don't like to separate action from objective. Acting—taking action—with an objective—purpose. The two are married completely and, with sincere apologies to Stanislavsky, talking about objective without talking about action is counterproductive. However, talking about action without talking about objective is quite productive. The idea of Stanislavsky's superobjective is a dangerous mischaracterization of what can serve to help an actor. Acting is not about objective at all. In the final analysis, acting, like life, is all about *taking action* and *listening*.

The Rehearsal Process

So, let's say you're an actor. You have a technique that you've been practicing. It consists of analyzing a play by scoring it (breaking it into beats and important phrases and key words); choosing, based on the text, how you use the presentational tools (where you need to take time and where you don't, where to go still, where to drive the tempo, and where to focus); and discerning the main action of your character and an action for each beat. Next, you've memorized the text, along with the score. (Actually, by the time you've analyzed it and made choices concerning the presentational tools, my bet is that you'll have most of the text committed to memory. It's difficult to do the kind of work I suggest and manage to avoid memorizing the text.) It would be most useful if you do all these things *before the first rehearsal*. That may seem like a radical statement, but in my experience, most actors don't memorize their lines for the first rehearsal. Most professional actors I'm familiar with certainly don't memorize their lines for the first rehearsal. Most actors of any type I've ever encountered don't even have their lines fully memorized two weeks before a show is scheduled to open. But you aren't like those actors. You, unlike all those other actors, are prepared.

In most first rehearsals, you will likely be required to read the scene out loud, most likely while sitting down. You may read it more than once. You probably will discuss, on some level, what's required in terms of staging. The director may actually stage it over the first few rehearsals. While it would be most useful if all the work I mentioned above was done at this point, it's not all really necessary. You wouldn't be able to concentrate on all of it anyway. However, it's preferable, for obvious reasons I hope, that you have your script scored before the first rehearsal. Because then, of course, you can *read the score*. Certainly, this would assist you in familiarizing yourself with *the plan you will execute*.

The second time you rehearse a scene, you should have the script completely scored and the text and score completely memorized. Then, as you rehearse, you should attempt to execute your *technical plan of the scene*. That is, know when to slow the tempo and when to build it; what the key words are and how you make them stand out from the rest of the text; when to move and when to be still; where to focus and when to change your focus. *Commit to your choices* and work with them throughout the rehearsal process, changing them as you go, if such changes are dictated by discoveries you make during the process.

It sounds like a lot, and it is. In the early part of the process, that's probably all you can concentrate on without driving yourself completely round the bend. You could, of course, just memorize the lines and go wing it. That's what a lot of actors out there seem to be doing. A lot of actors will take a text and "create" a bunch of "facts" that the playwright hasn't provided so that they then can "create" the character, as if the character is somehow separate from them. They don't pay a lot of attention to the actual text because the text is just a jumping-off point for their "creativity."

It might appear from the foregoing that I'm somehow against creativity. I'm not. Without question, when any group of theater practitioners produces a play, they bring the play "into being," and certainly that is the essence of "creation." The problem I have with the word "creativity" as it commonly is used in theatrical circles is that it has come to imply a "whole cloth" approach to theater. In other words, the playwright's text becomes secondary to the people producing the play. The play, rather than being a carefully considered, meticulously rendered story, is nothing more than an outline that the people producing it fill in. The playwright seemingly isn't a creator at all—the director, designers, and actors are the creators.

Nothing could be further from the truth. The truly effective director creates nothing except an atmosphere conducive to allowing the real workers—the designers and actors—to work effectively. The designers and actors—along with the playwright, the actual workers in the theater—should be focused strictly on rendering the truth that the playwright has provided. While there is certainly room for creativity in the theater, that creativity should come about not through what the participants *imagine* the playwright intended, but through what the playwright actually *provides*. Everyone in a theatrical process—director, designers, actors—should be focused on text-based choices. In fact, the director, if she's working effectively, should do only two things: organize the production and coach the actors. The director, if she's working effectively, should be nothing more or less than a filter between the real workers—the designers and actors—and the text of the playwright. In the theater, true creativity is being true to the creative source.

Outside of rehearsals, you should go over your lines as often as possible. Without the script. Without the cues. I can't tell you how many times I've heard actors complain about not having time to go over their lines, and I always find it amusing and, admittedly, more than somewhat frustrating. Throughout the course of any given day, almost endless possibilities to rehearse your lines will present themselves to you. When you shower. When you drive. When you're walking. When you're in the bathroom. Actors often hesitate to go over their lines in public places, but for crying out loud, who cares if people stare? Why should you care what people think of you? You're just doing your job. If strangers don't understand the job, what difference does that make? Should anyone approach you and ask if you're all right, you can always tell them that you're an actor and you're rehearsing your lines. Everyone will understand. Really. They will. Everyone understands what an actor does—or at least, they think they do.

As you near the midway point of the rehearsal process, you should have the technical execution of your plan down pat. During this phase of rehearsals, you really should work on little more than that—working as hard as you can to put your analysis onto the stage. Take mental notes as you rehearse about where you need to execute the plan more effectively, and work those notes hard outside of rehearsal. Get to know the plan you want to execute as well as you know the lines—and you'd better know the lines well, because if you don't know the lines like the back of your hand, how are you ever going to be able to know the plan?

All this time, lurking there in the background, are your actions. The ones you mapped out earlier in the process. The ones that are staring up at you every time you open your script (which should be often, and sooner rather than later). And as you've rehearsed, as you've played with the other actors, some of those actions might have changed. Before and after every rehearsal, in addition to going over your lines religiously, you should look at your actions and really consider them. Does the main action really cover everything you do as you tell the story? If it doesn't, then it's time to go back to the thesaurus (and the dictionary). Do the beat actions still work in the context of the rehearsal process? If not, then hit the books again. If, at any point in the process, a given action no longer seems to fit, then you need to find one that does. At the risk of getting ahead of myself, you need to play each of your chosen actions fully. Don't just write something down and then ignore it, and thus, forget about it. You should keep your actions, like your lines, under constant review. If you do, if you apply the technique consistently and have done the work I suggest, then as you move into the latter part of the rehearsal process, you will allow yourself the opportunity to *activate*.

Preparing to Activate

Activation consists of two parts: playing your action and listening.

Activating is being present in the scene (as opposed to being present in the theater). Activating is playing for the other actors (as opposed to playing for the audience). You may not like or care in any way for that person sitting across from you, acting with you. It's more advantageous, of course, if you do, but it isn't really necessary. No matter what kind of personal feelings you may have concerning your fellow actors, what you must do when you're onstage is *play for them*.

I talk to actors about playing for each other all the time, particularly at the end of a rehearsal process. A major component of becoming an effective actor is getting your focus off of things outside of your control and onto things that you can control— onto the stage.

Theater is live. It moves through time and space. Theater is not images projected on a screen (although we have them at our disposal, should we require them). Theater is not words on a page (although we have those in abundance). Theater is real, in every applicable sense of the word.

> **real** 1a: Being or occurring in fact or actuality; having verifiable existence 1b. True and actual; not imaginary, alleged, or ideal 1c. Of or founded on practical matters and concerns 2. Genuine and authentic; not artificial or spurious [Perhaps not what theater is, but certainly what it *should* be] 3. Being no less than what is stated; worthy of the name 4. Free of pretense, falsehood, or affectation [Again, perhaps not what theater is . . .] 5. Not to be taken lightly; serious 6. Existing objectively in the world regardless of subjectivity or conventions of thought or language [My favorite]

This is one set of definitions for the word "real," and every one of them applies to acting and, by extension, to theater. Yet I still run into people who argue that *theater isn't real*. When I set out my arguments, a common response, after much exasperation, is, "Oh come on, you know what I mean." But I don't.

Theater is real. As real as the life you live. The theater and life should be the same.

CHAPTER 18

Playing Your Action

RECENTLY AN ACTOR TOLD ME that she believed playing emotion and playing action were the same thing. I constantly find myself telling actors to play their actions fully, and this particular actor postulated that what I really was looking for when I made this request was a specific emotional state.

Of course, this isn't the case at all. Action is all about intent—"an aim or purpose, the state of one's mind at the time one carries out an action." Emotion is also defined as a mental state, but unlike intent, emotion "arises spontaneously rather than through conscious effort." (These are, in fact, the first definitions of the words "intent" and "emotion" that I found.) You can't play an emotion; it arises *spontaneously*, not consciously. In addition, if you attempt to play emotion, you'll direct your focus inward, and life simply doesn't work that way. In life, we work *outward*, toward others, through our *actions*.

Action is the most important tool in the actor's box because it's the thing that makes the house the actor builds interesting, and thus, beautiful and truthful. In a sense, the playwright's text is a framework, and when we analyze it, what we're doing is looking carefully at that frame, that structure. In other words, the playwright has put up the beams and the plumbing and the wiring, and even, in most cases, the walls and the roof. But the framework, and even the roof and the walls, is only interesting in the sense that you can see the shape of the house. There's nothing really living there—at least, not nearly enough to make it truly interesting—not in the flesh-and-blood sense. Can you imagine putting a script up on a stage, say, laying on a platform, or open on a podium or an easel, and having *that* be the entertainment? (We're in a Samuel Beckett play now. But don't get me wrong—I love Samuel Beckett.)

A script by itself, like the framework for a house, isn't interesting enough on its own to warrant the attention of an audience. But perhaps I didn't need to make that argument. Perhaps it's obvious that what holds the interest of an audience is an actor. An actor telling a story. An actor telling a story through the use of *action*.

Moving Toward Performance

Your beat actions assist you in making choices concerning the presentational tools as you move through the rehearsal process, and every one of those beat actions should relate directly to what you've discerned as your main action. However, as you near the end of the rehearsal process, you should begin to shift your focus away from your beat actions and concentrate almost solely on your main action.

Consider Macbeth's main action for his monologue: to control his fears. "To control" is a transitive verb, and the transitive verb is married to a set of objects. This is the essence of an effective main action. In addition, and as importantly, it applies to the *entire play*. Also note that the action statement, as it stands, doesn't provide an objective—*but it doesn't need one*. Marrying an objective to the action will do absolutely nothing to change its effectiveness. An argument could be made that "to control his fears" isn't an action statement at all—it's an objective. I would have to say that the argument has credence. But in the end, such an argument doesn't change a thing. "To control his fears" is *playable*; it assists an actor in presenting a character on a stage because it moves outward and implies strong physical and vocal tactics. Certainly, "to control his fears" is much more playable than "be more happy here" or "be more sad here." Using either of these emotional formulations, you're left doing little more than making faces. Audiences don't come to the theater to see actors making faces. They come to see *people in action*.

But wouldn't playing just one thing—one action—get a little boring? A little static? A little plain? Vanilla? Well, consider this: Is "to push him into vengeance" an action statement? It is, isn't it? Certainly, it's different from the *Macbeth* action statement because it's directed at a single object ("him") rather than a "set of objects," but there's no question that it's an action statement. Is it an effective one? Well, there may be only one other character in the play ("him"), and if that's the case, then we have an object. Is the verb "push" general enough to cover a range of actions? What does the verb "push" imply? Does it imply "persuade?" Impel? Propel? Put in motion? Urge? Prod? Shove? Strike, knock, hit, tap, rap, slap, flap, dab, pat, thump, beat, blow, bang, slam, dash, punch, thwack, whack, hit hard, strike hard, swap, batter, dowse, baste, pelt, patter, buffet, belabor, fetch one a blow, poke at, pink, lunge, kick, butt, strike at, attack, punish? While some of these verbs are much more effective than others for our purposes, there's little question that the verb "push" implies a wide range of actions. How much more effective is "to push him into vengeance" than "be more happy here?" How many more choices does "to push him into vengeance" offer than "be more happy here?"

What changes at a beat change? The story, certainly, but what aspect of the story? One part ends and another begins, but why does that happen? Because something shifts, yes? What? The *actions* of the characters. A beat changes because the characters' actions change (not the *character's* actions in the *singular*, but *all* the actions of *all* the characters). This would seem to imply that we need to write a different action for every beat of a play, and we do—the beat actions. But in terms of process, we need to keep our mind focused as simply as possible, and this is particularly so when we reach the end of rehearsals. We want to allow ourselves the room to focus in a *singular* manner, and the way to do that is to choose a main action that is broad enough to cover every action we take in the course of a story. This is, in fact, the way we operate in life. In life, consciously or unconsciously, we have a main action that we focus on, and we adjust that main action depending on the needs of the moment. In a sense, while our beat actions change in life, our main action remains the same, and the same should apply to the performance of a play. In performance, an actor shouldn't concentrate on the beat actions because it's not the main action that changes at a beat change so much as the *quality* of the main action, the *physical and vocal tactics* the character is utilizing for any given moment. We use the rehearsal process to ferret out those physical and vocal tactics.

When I refer to action, whether a main action or beat actions, I'm referring to what a character is doing on the deepest level possible. Not on the surface. The surface is obvious. "Action," as we use the term, is not simply a task—in other words, my "action" is to fill someone in on my background; to swear at someone; to explain something. These aren't actions. They're tasks. Each of these tasks is performed with something bigger, something deeper in mind—to impress someone; to antagonize someone; to amuse someone. Now, as always, the argument could be made that what I'm talking about with the latter are objectives, and I would argue, in turn, that it doesn't matter. If it's playable—that is, if it can be directed *at* another person—it's action. "To impress," "to antagonize," and "to amuse" are certainly all objectives in a sense, but they're actions as well. Each implies a particular set of physical and vocal tactics, and therefore, each is an action. Action-objective—chicken-egg. Makes no difference. If it's playable, it's action.

Action-Objective-Obstacle

In my early experience, particularly in academia, there was a grand triumvirate of acting: action-objective-obstacle. You did something to get something you wanted; something was standing in the way of what you wanted; you had to fight through that obstacle using your action. At no point in this text have I mentioned obstacle, not through design—I wish it had been—but because, in the final analysis, obstacle is obvious. Obstacle is that person onstage with you. That person who has something that you want. That person to whom you're going to do things to get what you want. One of the beauties of theater is that you always have to persuade that other to give you what you want—and that other almost never gives it to you. If that other does happen to give you something that you want, the giving of it only spurs you on to wanting more, and so you do more things to that other in an attempt to fill your newly acquired needs, wants, and desires. That other, in other words, is almost always your obstacle, and thus, almost always the object of your action. So it's not really necessary for you to find an object for your action. The object, in almost every case, is obvious—it's that other.

You might think, at this point, that executing everything I'm suggesting you need to execute is incredibly complicated. I mean, isn't there a lot to remember? Beats, key phrases, key words, beat actions, main action—it's too much, isn't it? It's a lot, admittedly, but fortunately, except in the most extreme cases, you always have time to rehearse, and you should use the rehearsal period in the way I've described: to make a detailed plan using every tool at your disposal. But as you near performance, you need to focus your concentration on something else.

You know that plan I keep referring to? How you make a plan and then you execute it? There's a reason I want you to work so hard on it. There's a reason I want you to know the plan as well as you know the text. The reason is so that you can *forget about it*. Well, not forget about it, not really—just *let it be*. Don't worry about it. Don't think about "what comes next."

If not that, if not the plan that you've spent so many hours of your life on, what is it that you need to think about?

Internal Monologue

Inside you, right now, there's an "internal monologue" progressing. A voice in your head. Listen to that voice (and if there is no voice in your head, then you're simply not listening hard enough). As most of you act, that voice is saying, "You look stupid. Don't do that. You sound dumb. Oh, that sounded good. Yeah, do that again." That voice is a long, drawn-out litany of judgment calls, none of which have anything to do with technique, all of which have to do with ego and vanity and prior influence and present corruption. For some of you, this is especially true— you're constantly outside yourselves, monitoring yourselves, judging yourselves, trying to look at yourself as others see you.

"Is everyone looking at me? Who's in the audience?" Your performance changes simply because someone new walks into the room for a brief moment. How many times has each of us seen *that* happen?

What does this mean in terms of performance? Like any other acting habit, in order to overcome it, you need to give some of your focus to it until you know it's gone. You need to listen—*really* listen—to what's going on in your own head. Monitor your internal monologue and *really* listen to what it's saying. If you find yourself judging yourself as others might judge you, find yourself making judgments of value and taste instead of judgments of craft, find yourself listening to the audience listen to you rather than doing what you should be doing—listening to the person speaking to you, the same way you listen in life—replace that self-centered mental mantra with the *mantra of action*. That's the reason we want a simple action statement. Our action statement is our *mantra*. That's what we need to concentrate on. Not the plan we make—we don't concentrate on the plan when we walk into our rooms every day. We concentrate on what we're doing (our action) and what that other person is doing (the other person's action) and how we might have to change what we're doing (our action) because of what that other person is doing (the other person's action) and . . . Whenever you feel lost onstage, whenever your internal monologue is carrying you away from the scene and out into the audience—out into the world—you should simply flick a switch in your head and concentrate on what you need to be doing. Concentrate on your *action*. Not the world. The world is what messed you up to begin with. To *hell* with the world.

Just do what you do. *Really* do it.

Listening

THE MOST BLATANT EXAMPLES OF INEFFECTIVE FOCUS can
be found by observing many actors "listen" onstage. I once heard
a director say of an actor, "I love him. He's such an active
listener." I saw this particular actor perform. He was exactly as
he was described. He moved his face and body constantly while
other actors were speaking. Rarely was there a moment in which
he wasn't moving, and often his movement had little to do with
what the other actors were saying. In other words, rather than
being an accompaniment to his fellow actors' performances, his
movement was a performance all by itself, having little to do
with anything happening around him. When he was onstage
"listening," the audience's concentration was drawn to him,
and they completely lost the thread of the story. The audience
was so occupied watching him listen that they couldn't concentrate on what the other actors were saying.

The theater should be no different from life. In life, when we
listen, we almost invariably move only to have an effect on the
speaker. Watch people listening to others and you'll see that this
is true. In a sense, the listener accompanies the speaker. If the
listener moves, the movement is almost always small and unno-
ticeable, at least in a way that an audience would recognize
consciously, and the listener focuses almost exclusively on and
accompanies the rhythm of the speaker.

If an actor is speaking, chances are the speaking actor is
meant to be the primary focal point of the scene. Anyone else
onstage should focus on the speaker. Everyone present should listen to what the speaker is saying—or, at the very least, they
should pay lip service to listening to the speaker. That means they

should focus on the speaker, whether they're actually listening or not. If you do this, you may feel like you're "doing nothing." I mean, if you're just standing there, focusing on the speaker, you must be "doing nothing," right? *Wrong.* You're *listening.* Better yet—you're reconnoitering. Or evaluating. Or watching. Or performing some other action that will, at the very least, keep you active mentally and directed outwardly toward the speaker during the scene. But if you're incapable or unequipped to play an action while remaining basically still, just *listen.* Like you listen in life. If you must "do" something while you're listening—in other words, engage in physical movement of some kind—then do the kinds of things you do in life. If you must do something, do very *small,* very *simple* things. And only do things that will accompany and support the speaker. In other words, *listen technically.* Only do things *on the speaker's rhythm.* Whatever you do, be *very selective* about it. Never do anything that will draw undue focus. Because if stories were meant to be about people listening, there would be no stories at all.

Now, I'd much rather you actually listen. Listen the same way you do in life: in order to interact. Action and listening are the keys to truly effective acting because they're the primary things we do when interacting in life. The *interaction* that comes about through playing action and listening is, in fact, the key to truly effective theatrical acting. I have immense distaste for the word "react," and with good reason—it leads to indication. It leads to telling the audience, "See? I'm listening now. You can tell by the way I'm *reacting* to what the speaker is saying." "React" implies an acting on one's own.

In life, we don't move only for the sake of moving. Our movement always has purpose. Our movement is always directed at someone or something, often even when we're alone. I don't make beds and do dishes because I necessarily enjoy it; I do it because it pleases my spouse and my children, who in turn please me with their response. I make beds and do dishes because it has an *effect on other people.* Does this make me a cynic? Possibly. More importantly, it illustrates the idea that our actions, even when we're alone, often are directed outwardly, not inwardly. While there are scenes in the theater that suggest an action should be directed inwardly, they are the vast exception to the rule, like scenes in which one character ignores another.

On first consideration, it may be difficult to accept the idea of listening on the stage. After all, we've made this plan and, in order to execute it, we have to give part of our mental attention to it, don't we? But if you've done the work, if you've used the rehearsal process to prepare yourself thoroughly, if you know the plan you're to execute as well as—no, hopefully better than— you know yourself, you shouldn't have to give your focus to it in performance. If you know the plan you're to execute as well as you know yourself, you won't *have* to focus on it. You can focus on the things you focus on in life: acting on others and listening as others act on you.

Of course, if you give yourself over to listening onstage— really listening, not just waiting for a cue—then you run the risk of forgetting what comes next. But what comes next should not be your concern in performance—only in the earlier stages of rehearsal. In performance, the theater should work the same way life works because it *is* life, a reflection of the eternal patterns that make up the truth of life. In life, we don't know what comes next. We cannot *anticipate* what comes next (although actors on the stage often anticipate what comes next—because they aren't *listening*). In life, we may have an expectation of what comes next, but true knowledge eludes us. If the theater and life are to be the same, are to work the same way (and they should), we shouldn't anticipate anything. We should simply make plans and execute them, and whatever happens, happens.

In life, we interact. We should in the theater as well.

CHAPTER 20

Playing for Each Other

ONE OF MY OLDEST FRIENDS IS A CYNIC. He believes that all people are out for themselves. He believes that people take action only for their own pleasure, for their own gratification. He is not the only person who believes these things.

I believe that all characters in plays, with a few exceptions, are out for themselves. They behave exactly according to the beliefs of my friend. They do everything for their own pleasure, to manipulate situations to their advantage, to manipulate *other people* to do their bidding, for no other reason than to help them satisfy their own needs, wants, and desires.

Earlier I wrote about my belief that, when they were young, many actors, if not all of them, became actors because some essential intimacy was denied them. While it's certain that actors aren't the only people seeking intimacy, unlike most people, actors, and even other performers, are seeking intimacy in a very special way. They aren't looking to control simply the person they happen to be talking to at any given moment. They seek an arranged situation in which they have the opportunity to control the attention *of an entire group of people*. And that group of people pays money to see them make the attempt.

I believe that's a cynic's description of theater. This is mine: Theater is where people come to experience eternal truth.

Theater sprang from ritual, and ritual sprang from the human need to connect to the eternal, to the earth, the oceans, the sun, moon, stars, to nature eternal and entire. Interconnection was, at one time, a deeply embedded fact of life. Like any religion, theater was a ritualized expression of people's need to experience the eternal.

When I say that an actor has the greatest responsibility a person can shoulder, I'm not exaggerating. When you step on the stage, you are responsible for at least two human lives—your own and your character's. In fact, you are your character, in the same way that you are yourself.

But you're more than that as well. You are the priest. You are the vessel filled by the story. You are the conduit between the audience and the everlasting.

You are the shaman who plays the drum.

That's the theater I'm looking for. I think it worthy of awesome effort.

It begins and ends with the actor. Any actor has an advantage over the priest. While the priest is stuck repeating the same old stories, we have hundreds of texts from which to choose. While the priest is confined to a prescribed space, we can create the space in which we perform. While the priest must be himself, we can be anyone we need to be.

Our advantages are great, but the priest has one that, at first glance, we can't match. He has ancient texts from which fanatic followers have sprung. He has a built-in audience. Has for years. Will have for years. He has God on his side. But an actor, an experienced actor, one who understands story and has given herself to the craft, and thus, to the art, has something even more persuasive and powerful on her side: She has Truth.

What I'm most interested in is connection. The kind of work I'm suggesting you do is work you do on yourself, by yourself, without anyone's help. But finally, you still have to deal with that person sitting across from you. That other. Chances are excellent that the person you're acting with is someone approaching theater in a cynical way. That other person's head is in the audience. How, exactly, are you going to take this plan you've made and go out and execute it, when you have little idea of what this other person might do?

Well, what can you do? You can approach it cynically. You can focus entirely on yourself and your presentation, standing outside yourself and judging yourself, waiting for the other person to finish saying his line so you can say your line. You can match him, ego for ego. In fact, you probably can dominate him, given that you have technique on your side and the other actor most likely doesn't. But then what would you be? Another cynical actor. Another actor with her head in the audience.

Or you can do exactly what every other living human being on the face of the earth is doing: You can seek intimacy. Connection.

When I say to make a detailed plan, I mean exactly that. The plan I suggest you make allows you to walk on the stage with tremendous confidence. But that's not how we approach life. If the theater is to be a true reflection of life—of the truth not just about human beings, but of *life*—an actor should not walk onto the stage feeling entirely safe. If one thing is certain, it is that nothing is safe in this man's world. To truly reflect life, actors should not feel entirely safe.

I often say that when you walk on the stage, you should forget the plan, but I don't really mean that. Assume that the plan is there for your use. Don't worry about it, don't give your attention to it, don't even think about it. Go out onstage and try to *do* something to that other person. And when that other person speaks, *listen*. Don't think about what comes next. You don't know what comes next in life. You may have an expectation—but again, the theater and life are the same. See it?

If the theater is to be a true reflection of life, then the actor must seek intimacy in the same way as she does in life. It's that simple.

Now, you could say the theater isn't like life. After all, a bunch of people sit and watch you.

That's right.

The audience is one of the purest things about the theater because the audience is there for the reason that the actors *should* be there, but usually are not: to experience eternal truth.

I can hear someone shouting, "Ah, what a bunch of bull. The audience just wants to be entertained."

Well, what could be more entertaining than experiencing eternal truth?

So how should an actor handle the audience? What should an actor's approach to the audience be? Same as always—the same way as in life. In life, we are constantly being observed, and are observing. Sometimes, we even think of the people we're speaking to as our audience. (All the time?) Whoever's listening to us, or watching us—they're our audience. Certainly, the theater presents a much more formal arrangement than usual, but the theater and life are the same.

Or should be.

Assuming that all of this is true—and that's a big assumption, isn't it?—that theater is a direct link to eternal truth, to the possibility of exchange, intimacy, and connection, how can you trust that the person you're acting with will stay with you on the stage, keep his head out of the audience and be present with you, striving toward the possibility of an exchange, of intimacy, of connection? Just because you are, how can you know that the other person is doing the same?

Think of it this way: How can you continue to go through life trusting that the person you're with at any given time is present with you, striving toward the possibility of an exchange, of intimacy, of connection?

If actors wish to be truthful in the theater, to allow connection with the eternal, and to allow the audience the same—since that is exactly what they've come for—then actors must play for each other. The same way we play for each other in life.

Hey, give it a shot. Something might *happen*.

CHAPTER 21

Emotion

tool 3 : an instrument or apparatus used in performing an
operation or needed in the practice of a vocation or profession.

I'VE OFTEN SAID—PROBABLY TOO OFTEN—that emotion is
not a tool and that the problem with most modern acting theory
is that emotion is postulated as a tool. I say this because it's true:
If you even *imply* that emotion is something that can be utilized
to aid in an effective performance, then you imply, whether you
state it directly or not, that emotion is a tool. (See that definition
for "tool" immediately above? A "tool" is "used." In other words,
a tool can be concretely manipulated, can be "utilized.")

I'm not saying that emotion isn't useful. It is, but it can't
be *used*. It just happens. It just occurs. And if it does happen
to occur—if you're presenting a role and suddenly begin to
feel what, either through analysis or through intuition, you
believe the character should be feeling, *that's fantastic*. That's
useful. But you don't need it. The audience doesn't care what
you're feeling. It can't see that. It cares only about what
you're doing. *That* it can see. And since the audience is the
reason that we tell stories to begin with, we should focus solely on what they've come to see, which is people doing things
to other people.

While I agree that discussing what a character is feeling can
on occasion be useful, I agree only with this caveat: That seems to
be all that actors do. Recently I privately auditioned two actors
who, because of schedule conflicts, could not attend a public audition. One was a twelve-year-old boy, and one was a thirty-one-
year-old woman. Each presented a prepared monologue for me.

I then gave each a monologue to read out loud, from the play for which they were auditioning. I gave both an opportunity to review their respective monologues, and then I asked each to read the monologue for me, taking each aside so that both could feel like they were reading to me privately. Before the boy began, he asked, "So, what are you looking for here? Do you want me to be irritated? Do you want me to be angry? Upset?" When I took the woman aside, *she did exactly the same thing. She asked exactly the same types of questions.* Two people of different genders, different ages, and, safe to assume, different backgrounds and experiences; yet both, when given an opportunity to ask a director about the presentation of an unfamiliar piece of text, went immediately for an emotional state of being to assist them in their presentation.

Every time I see an actor interviewed on television about a role, almost everything that comes out of that actor's mouth concerns emotional states of being. Whenever I hear actors outside the workshop discussing characters or performances, almost everything I hear them discuss relates to emotion. Actors are addicted to talking about characters in emotional terms. It may very well be that all these actors were instructed by teachers who never mentioned emotional states of being, but if that were the case, why do these actors discuss everything about a character in strictly emotional terms, as if emotion is the first and last tool of the actor?

Why? Because it's *easy*. It's certainly much easier—and those of us working the technique advocated herein know this intimately—than talking about what a character is actually *doing*. Discerning action is the most difficult thing about analysis. Playing an action—activating a performance—is more challenging still. Because we're so addicted, not just as actors, but as people, to discussing our feelings, our states of being, our attitudes, our *emotions*, I suggest that, if we wish to kick the habit, we do what the heroin user does: quit cold-turkey. Before we allow ourselves to refer to emotion or attitude or a state of being in terms of either something we're tasked to play or something we've seen played, we discuss it only in terms of action. Difficult? Yes, most certainly. Rewarding? Off the scale.

If you want to change the way you act, change the way you talk about acting, because in order to change the way you talk about acting, you have to change the way you think about acting. When discussing acting, do not allow words describing an emotional state of being to pass your lips.

CHAPTER 22

Why We Are Afraid

> I wanted to write a poem
> that you would understand.
> For what good is it to me
> if you can't understand it?
> But you got to try hard . . .
>
> —William Carlos Williams, "January Morning"

I am afraid.

And you should be too. For what can be known? With certainty? Where can we turn for truth?

This book came about because of an acting workshop I lead. The workshop was initiated with a clearly articulated purpose: to elucidate a technique of acting that could be applied to any given text. I didn't believe that such a thing—that a clear and concise lexicon of acting—was then in existence. Certainly there were excellent texts about acting, but not one I believed presented all the fundamental tools that an actor absolutely needed to understand in order to present text effectively, and did it in an understandable and immediately applicable way. I believed that, by finding examples of effective acting and then deducing the mechanisms that supported these effective presentations, an observer could appropriate those mechanisms—those tools—and sort of reverse-engineer. That is, observers could apply the mechanisms—tools—to given texts, and in turn, become effective actors themselves.

And it worked. It took some time, of course, but it worked. Consistently applied, the technique advocated herein works with total novices and with the greatly experienced, because it is founded on tools that can be easily controlled and manipulated. Through the utilization of those tools, it requires the individual actor to keep her focus squarely on the stage, with her fellow actors.

None of which is to say that all of this happens immediately. On the contrary, it takes time—more time for some, less for others—but for anyone who works at it, no matter what her level of experience, the technique leads to effective acting relatively quickly, often in weeks, not in months or years. My wife, who teaches high school theater, has found that simply making her young, callow students aware of the utilization and manipulation of focus and stillness leads to tremendous and immediate improvement in their presentation. If you're within the range of normal—young or old—you give yourself to the technique, and you work hard, you can act effectively on a consistent basis.

Now, it could very well be that I'm ignorant. In fact, I'm fond of saying more or less exactly that. I certainly have been ignorant in the past, and most probably will be again in the future, if I'm not so now in the present. It could be that, if an actor simply works hard, memorizes a lot of text, and goes out on the stage and presents it, she could achieve results similar to those that have been achieved in my workshop. It could very well be— but it's highly unlikely, because if that were the case, most of the acting I see would work. But it doesn't.

For a considerable amount of time I've been pondering why the technique outlined herein seems to work so well, so consistently, and so quickly—much more consistently and quickly than any other acting technique I've ever encountered—and the conclusion I've come to is that it works the way it does simply because it requires actors to speak the way people speak in life. I often suggest that actors go to a mall to watch and, if possible, listen to people speak. *Observe* the way they speak. Better yet, listen to the radio, to all those talking heads (or talking voices, as the case may be). Radio is an effective thing for an actor to listen to because the people speaking know they aren't being observed and therefore do not "act" for the observer; rather, they know people are listening, not watching, and therefore try to make themselves clear in a strictly vocal way. As those talking voices begin a new thought, they almost invariably use a slow tempo. As they expound on that thought—enlarge upon it, *build* on it—they increase their tempo, and often their volume, building to their point, which comes at the height—the climax—of their vocal pattern. As they finish their thought, they often slow down as they come to the end, possibly to cue the other speaker—if there is another speaker—that it's now his turn to speak, and thus, to repeat the pattern. Listen to commercials on the radio. The names of businesses, the selling points—the tempo for these is *slowed*. The technique at which we have arrived isn't a technique at all. It's simply the way people speak.

Of course, you have to take someone else's words and make them your own. And to a certain extent, that's what all this is really about. Making something your own. (Making your *self* your own.) And the way to do that is to speak the way people speak (the way *you* speak) and to do the things people do (the things *you* do). Every character is a person; in fact, your character is you. As much as—*more than*—you are yourself.

I'm afraid, and I know what it is I fear. It's the unknown. You—I can't know you, truly know you, no matter how hard I try. The nature of the world—I can't know that either, not truly and with certainty. We are strangers to each other and to the world, and always will be. But there is something that can be known, if only we really wish to look. It is *ourselves*. You can know *yourself*. You may not want to, and I can't say I blame you. For in order to know yourself, you may have to face things buried so deep you did not know they existed, and those things may be frightening—terribly, horribly frightening. But what I suggest is not rejection of the past, turning away from it, or even reconciliation with it. Simply examination. Acknowledgment. Look in the mirror. Do you like what you see? If you do, then whatever has happened is, in a sense, all good, and you can look at it all. It won't harm you. It's made you what you are, and *you* are good. But if you look in the mirror and don't like what you see, you can *change*. Just examine yourself. Know yourself, though you may be unknown. Certainly, the unknown is fraught with fear, but it is our fear that in many ways makes us most human. Perhaps it's not fear that you're feeling, but excitement. Seek the truth of yourself, for if stories are what you wish to tell, it is the truth of yourself that you seek—and the truth will set you *free*.

PART 4

Other Useful Stuff

CHAPTER 23

Auditioning

THERE ARE WHOLE BOOKS OUT THERE ABOUT AUDITIONING. (Given that you're reading this, I probably don't have to tell you that.) But for me, auditioning is pretty simple and doesn't require a book. Don't get me wrong—there's useful information in those books.

I once directed a musical for a local university. A sophomore theater major came to the auditions, which consisted of singing sixteen bars of a song and performing a one-minute monologue from a musical or a comedy. She sang her song and was quite effective. She then told me that she was going to perform the role of Puck from *A Midsummer Night's Dream*, and proceeded to take a sheet of paper out of a pocket. She looked at the paper, put it down on the piano, faced me, and began her monologue. About three or four lines in, she forgot her next line, stopped, took a look at the paper, apologized, and asked if she could start over.

This is *not* the way you want to audition.

The Five Hard-and-Fast Rules of Auditioning

As with many of my previous rules, these may appear obvious. But I hope you've gathered by now that my method is not merely madness. So here are the rules for auditioning:

- Be prepared
- Have a variety of audition pieces at your disposal
- Audition to work, not to impress

- Play it by ear
- Expect nothing

Now that we've seen the rules in their simple glory, let's look at each one of these in a bit more detail.

Be Prepared

In other words, rule number one means know what you're going to do and how you're going to do it. Don't just memorize the pieces and go in and wing it. Memorize the pieces and make a plan, the same way you would with any presentation. Plan everything, every gesture, every pause, every nuance, right down to the batting of an eyelash. Have a résumé and photo available, whether they're required or not. Take a pencil (not a pen, not a marker, not a crayon—a pencil). Dress informally but not sloppily. (You may have to dance or move in some strange fashion—there's no telling what a director might ask you to do. And don't show a lot of skin unless you want the audition to be about your chest or your belly or your legs. If that's what you want it to be about, then by all means, go in there naked. That'll make a statement.) Practice good hygiene. (Don't stink, but don't smell like a room full of flowers either. Make sure you brush your teeth.) It all sounds pretty obvious, doesn't it? You'd be surprised.

Have a Variety of Audition Pieces At Your Disposal

Have at least the following pieces at your disposal: a Shakespeare piece; a dramatic piece (not Shakespeare); a comic piece; and a song that you can sing effectively (with or without accompaniment). Notice I didn't say "sing well." Anyone can sing, whether they can carry a tune or not. Songs are just stories with really cool rhythm and really specific pitch and resonance. It's all in the presentation. But you really should have more than that. You should have so many pieces that you can overwhelm the director with choices. When I'm preparing to audition, I have at least ten pieces I can present, and that includes two songs. Why so many pieces? Let me put it this way: If you're an athlete and you're asked by a coach to run forty yards with a group of other athletes, do you just run nice and easy and take your time, or do you run hard and fast and try to beat every other person in the group? Which style of running says more about you as an individual? Which says more about what you value? Which says more about what you're willing to do? Not to go on and on about it, but which is going to be more impressive? (And please don't accuse me of trying to turn acting into a competition, because there's no denying the competitive aspect of an audition.)

You may think that you're never going to need all those pieces. And you may not. You may never get to use them all. But a good friend of mine who was about to audition for graduate schools asked me for audition advice, and I gave him exactly what I'm giving you. I helped him prepare eight or ten pieces, I can't remember how many, and at one of his auditions—and only one of them—he went in and did what was required, and then was asked, "Have you got anything else?"

He said, "Well, yeah, I've got this other piece."

"Okay, do that."

He did, and was asked again and again until he'd gone through everything that he'd prepared. That was his audition for Yale, and that's where he was accepted. I'm not saying that if you're all well prepared you're going to end up at Yale, but I think you get the point.

Audition to Work, Not to Impress

If your aim is to impress the people you're auditioning for, you may succeed, but you'll run into the same problem that 99.9 percent of actors suffer from: You'll have your head in the audience. You should treat the audition process the same way you treat the performance process or the classroom process or any other process that involves acting: Treat it as work. Treat every opportunity to act as an opportunity to *work*, to *tune your instrument*, to *exercise your creative instincts*. To work on your *self*. If you're working to impress, your focus will be outside yourself and you won't be able to focus on what you really need to focus on in order to obtain the kind of success you seek: *execution*.

Play It By Ear

You never know what's going to happen at an audition, which is why you should be totally prepared. If you're totally prepared, you can make any adjustments you need to make and, when given the opportunity, simply return to what you prepared. For instance, people are going to ask you questions. Answer them honestly. Don't try to ferret out why the questions are being asked. Don't vacillate. Don't ever *ever* lie at an audition. (Your word should be sacred. Lying, generally speaking, is very bad policy.) In the short term, you may gain an advantage. In the long term, you're going to hurt yourself. If the director, or whomever you're auditioning for, asks you to do something, listen very carefully and do exactly what is asked of you to the best of your ability. Pay close attention here: *Listen very carefully and do exactly what is asked of you to the best of your ability.* This takes concentration and commitment on your part, the same kind of concentration and commitment it takes to act effectively. If you're thinking, "I hope they like me, I hope they like me," or if you're thinking about your last piece and how you blew it, you're never going to hear what you're being asked to do and you're going to mess it up. Or, almost as bad, you're going to change things that the director didn't want you to change. *Listen carefully whenever anyone speaks to you, and do exactly what is asked of you to the best of your ability.*

Expect Nothing

Expect nothing—this one is self-explanatory. And it's a good life rule as well. On second thought, you should expect one thing: that you'll do the best you can under the circumstances. If you expect only that, then you'll keep your disappointments to a minimum.

Those five rules are hard-and-fast rules.

Audition Structure

I'm providing the following audition structure as a general guideline of events, as they would happen, in chronological order.

Introduce Yourself

Speak loudly and clearly—remember the prerequisites of effective acting—and tell everyone your name. Believe it or not, telling people your name is one of the most important, if not *the* most important, parts of your audition, so make sure you take your time and say it so that everyone can understand it. Smile as you introduce yourself and your pieces. You catch more bees with honey.

Introduce Your Pieces

Different people prefer different ways, but you should know the titles of the plays your pieces are from, the authors of the plays, and the names of the characters you're portraying. (If it's a Shakespeare piece, you might want to know the act and scene, but if a director is asking you for these, he's got his head in the wrong place anyway, and you most likely don't want to work with him.) You should also know how to *pronounce everything correctly.* If you're at all unsure about how to pronounce something, ask someone whom you believe is an authority and will be able to provide you with the correct pronunciation.

Prepare Yourself

Before you begin your first piece, take a moment to *prepare yourself mentally.* Try doing the following: Put your head down and focus on your key.

How best to describe what I mean by saying, "Put your head down"? It may sound simple, but actors have a way of complicating even the simplest things, because their minds are so often squarely in the audience. I had an actor once who put her head down by first lifting up her chin slightly, as if she were going to look at the ceiling, and then slowly letting her head down so that her chin was resting close to the top of her chest. In other words, she didn't just "put her head down," she *placed* her head down. Don't *place* your head. Just drop it. If you're not comfortable "putting your head down," then try just dropping your chin slightly, like you're nodding, and letting your eyes focus down. It's the same thing.

So, after you finish your introduction, *drop your head*. Once you've managed to drop your head, focus on your "key"—not a key phrase or word, but a "key" as in "a key to unlock the scene." Find an action or a phrase or a gesture or a tempo or a rhythm that you can think about that will help "key" you into the scene and get you off on the right foot. Because, believe it or not, it's *always* possible to get off on the right foot. Once you've focused on your key, lift your head and begin your monologue. Once you've finished your monologue, let the stillness hold for a moment, and then drop your head again.

If Doing More Than One Piece, Prepare Yourself Again

If you're required to present only one piece, go to the next heading. If you're presenting two pieces, then after you finish the first, take a moment again and *prepare for your next piece*. Notice that I haven't said to "relax." Yes, absolutely, you should relax, but do not outwardly relax unless you absolutely must. In other words, don't sigh, shake yourself all over like a dog coming out of the water, and then lift your head and begin your next piece. If you're an actor— and if you're reading this, then guess what?—you should have a place you can go to in your head that will allow you to *automatically relax your instrument*. There should be a place in your head you can go to that will allow you to locate any tension you have in your instrument and release it. Once you've done this, focus on the key for your next piece and present it.

Make sure your stage is set before you do your introduction. The two most common audition setups are an empty stage—just you standing there—and a stage with a chair on it. If there's a chair on the stage and you don't require it, move it off to the side before you do your introduction. If you need a chair and one isn't present on the stage, ask for one. If a chair is there and you need a chair for your audition, make sure it's set where you want it, and then introduce yourself. If you're doing your first piece standing and you need a chair for the second piece, keep the chair off to the side for the first piece, and then set the chair before you do the introduction for your second piece.

Be Nice and Polite (In Other Words, Charm Everyone)

After you've finished your final monologue (or your only monologue, as the case may be), raise your head, smile, loudly and clearly say, "Thank you," and leave. Someone may stop you and ask you to stay and answer questions, or even to do another piece or read from a script. If they do, do what's asked. If they don't, hit the road (hopefully evaluating your presentation in a brutal fashion as you go). If they ask you questions, don't assume anything. Just follow Hard-and-Fast Rule #4 and remember Hard-and-Fast Rule #5—expect nothing.

To return to the young lady who blew her audition. After she asked if she could start again, I told her no, she couldn't. (Most any director can see everything he needs to see after about fifteen seconds of an audition—all the more reason for you to nail the beginning of whatever you're doing. In any audition, I ask for more than fifteen seconds of acting because I want everyone to feel they've had a fair chance. Admittedly, some have caught my eye late in an audition, but not often.) I didn't yell at her or raise my voice. I told her that she shortchanged herself and her talent (and she was talented—not greatly, but she had presence, could relax, and had a pleasant voice) by coming to an audition in such an unprepared manner. I told her that there are people out there who would have no patience for an actor who would come to an audition and do what she did; that the next time she came to an audition she should have not just one, but multiple pieces to perform; and that she should know each like the back of her hand. I told her that she should never put herself or the people she's auditioning for in that kind of position again. Then I released her. She took it very well. Always take it—whatever "it" is—very well. Don't burn any bridges unless someone is actually abusing you. Then feel free to squash them totally.

And yes, she got cast.

CHAPTER 24

Cold Reading

IF YOU GO TO AN AUDITION OR A CALLBACK that consists of
cold readings, what is it you're given to read? A *text*, correct? And
any given text lends itself to what? *Analysis.*

Cold readings are never actually "cold." To me, "cold" would
be if you weren't given a chance to sit down and look at the
scene, but rather, were given it and immediately shoved up in
front of folks to read it. Now, *that's* cold—in more ways than one.
But I don't think I've ever seen that happen at an audition. You
are *always* given a chance to read a scene silently before you have
to read it aloud.

Scoring a Cold Reading

What you'll be required to do at a cold reading audition is to *paint
fast.* Pay attention, because here comes the reason why you
should always bring a pencil to an audition: When you get the
opportunity to sit down and read that scene silently, don't just
read it, *score it.* As you read the scene, at a minimum, mark where
you think the beats are. If you have time, mark what appear to
be the key phrases—but that isn't really necessary. More importantly, try to get some kind of handle on what you think the
main action of the scene is for the character you're reading.
Then, when you're called in to read, *read the score.* It may be that
you didn't have time to mark much more than the beats, but
that's okay, because since you're experienced in analyzing text,
you know the most important information is going to be right
around the beat changes. Trust your effective storytelling
instincts. Drive through the middles of beats, take time with

phrases around the beats, go still at any beat change you control, and play your chosen action (if you've chosen an action) fully. As much as possible, treat the cold reading just like it's a performance of a prepared piece. Prepared or cold—it's all just storytelling. It all works the same way.

You might say, "Hey, Barry, shouldn't I be trying to get to know the scene before I read it? Because no one in his right mind approaches a cold reading this way, do they?"

And I would respond: That's right. They don't. And you *are* getting to know it. What do you think you're doing when you score it? To some degree, all writing is formulaic. You're just deducing the formula. You're *analyzing* it. You're *becoming intimate* with it. And if you approach a cold reading this way, you'll have an advantage over everyone else there. They'll be flying by the seats of their pants. They'll be trying to impress the director or whomever. They'll be standing outside themselves, watching themselves and judging themselves. You won't be. You'll be working.

Obviously, if you have the opportunity to get the script beforehand, you're at a tremendous advantage, compared to your average actor. Your average actor will read it, and then, maybe, reread it, all the time trying to think of ways to impress the director. You, on the other hand, will simply do your work and then execute.

When you score your side (the copy of the scene), you should try to do so out of sight of the people running the audition, since you don't want to upset them by writing on their sides. However, chances are they're using photocopies of single scenes for the audition, so you can probably feel free to write in it, since it's just going to be used for scrap or, like so much in our culture, discarded after it has served its purpose. After you've used it and returned it, if any other actors happen to see your score, they won't know what all those pencil marks mean anyway, and they'll just ignore them.

On the other hand, maybe they won't ignore them. If they're of above-average intelligence, they'll probably have a good idea of what someone was doing with all those pencil marks. Scoring is, after all, very much like making a map, and anybody can follow a simple set of directions. Think about this: Any two people, if they understand the technique, can perform exactly the same score in exactly the same way. Most people would tell you that what will be different is their *interpretation*, but as I'm fond of saying, "interpretation" is a word that the ignorant use to bludgeon the thoughtful. What would be different is not their *interpretation*, but the simple fact that they are *different people*. Score— same. People—different. Interpretation—utter horsepucky.

Should someone ask you to stop writing in the side (or the script, if you haven't been given a side), you have an automatic out if you show them that you're *scoring it lightly* and you promise to *erase it afterwards*. But whatever you do, don't ask permission— just write in it. There are more than a few people out there on such incredible power trips that they won't give you permission to write on a photocopy of a script, even when they're just going to throw it away. So don't ever ask. Just do it and apologize later, if you should have to.

Presenting a Cold Score

As for the cold reading itself, as you read your score, you should try as much as possible to "work out of the script." In other words, make eye contact with the actors with whom you're reading. But don't ever do this at the expense of the story. You're there to serve the story, period—not the director, and certainly not the other actors.

It's easiest to work out of the script at the ends of the lines and at beat changes. (Be careful about doing it in the middle of a line or speech unless you're really sure of yourself, because if you stumble, you'll look foolish.) You should try to work out of your script for a couple of reasons: (1) It makes you seem eager; and (2) Directors like to see actors trying to connect. However—and this is going to sound radical, but I believe this with all my heart—you should make no actual attempt to connect with anyone you're auditioning with. Only pay lip service to it. Cold readings are a competitive situation, plain and simple. You're competing with every other actor there for a role. You won't be able to compete with some of them. Some of them will be better for some of the roles than you. Some of them will be more talented than you. Some of them may even be more skilled than you. But if you understand and execute the technique outlined herein, I sincerely doubt that.

Take Advantage of Your Opportunities

If you're being asked to read cold from a script, you probably already auditioned and got called back. And if that's the case, you can take this to the bank and make a nice, fat deposit: If you weren't being considered for a role, you wouldn't have gotten a callback. The people casting don't want to waste their time. If you're politically correct—if you know someone important or have a certain stature in your theater community—then it's possible you might get a callback simply for appearance's sake. But generally speaking, people casting a play aren't interested in wasting their time looking at people they have no intention of casting. If you get called back, you're being considered. Which, of course, means you should take the opportunity to blow everyone else at the audition away. And how do you do this? By *being prepared*. If you can get the script ahead of time, get it and score it and get to know it well. If you can't get the script ahead of time, get it when you can and score it quick and dirty. Either way, you're going to be way ahead of 99 percent of the actors auditioning.

And if you don't get cast? Well, it doesn't really matter. What matters is *the work*. Do the work and, chances are you *will* blow everyone else at the audition away. You may not get cast, but that's not in your control. What *is* in your control is the work you do. If you don't get cast, what you did get was a further opportunity to tune your instrument. Do the work, and eventually—probably sooner rather than later—everything will take care of itself.

Some Final Cold Reading Suggestions

A couple of final suggestions: Dress as you would for a monologue audition, paying attention to any special requirements (like the "you may be asked to move" requirement, one that never ceases to elicit a smile from me—I mean, are you ever asked *not* to move?). Pay attention to personal hygiene (always). If someone in charge speaks to you and asks you to do something while you're auditioning, listen carefully and do exactly what is asked to the best of your ability. Just like any other audition.

Smile, as much and as often as possible. If spoken to, keep your responses to a minimum while answering any question fully. And lastly, and most importantly, if you have questions, ask them. You should always control what you can control, and one of the things you can control is your knowledge of the requirements of the audition. In other words, if someone gives you a hundred lines of Shakespeare verse to read, you might want to ask, "Am I going to be reading all of this?" Make sure you know exactly what it is you're going to be asked to read, or you'll never know what it is you're going to need to score. Auditioning is all about preparation, and it's always possible to be prepared.

CHAPTER 25

Taking Direction

IN REHEARSAL, ACTORS SHOULD BE SEEN AND, except for their lines, not heard. It's not that I think an actor shouldn't ask questions, but for the most part, an actor should "do," not "talk." If you've memorized your lines—and not just memorized them, but made your lines habitual, made them a part of you the same way brushing your teeth and showering and making your bed and a hundred other habits are a part of you, a part of you so that you can whip them off without the cues, and you've done this before you ever walk through the door for rehearsal—then you'll rarely have a need to say anything in rehearsal except your lines.

I recently had an actor say to me, "What's my relationship to this other character?" What a waste of time—mine and the actor's! You want a director to define your relationship to the other characters? Would you like the director then to tell you what your action is? To tell you where to focus? To tell you when to gesture? It's not that any of these aren't within the purview of the director—everything about the production is within the purview of the director—but if you'd like the director to dictate the answers to such all-important questions as relationship and action and focus, why not let the director just spoon-feed you the entire performance? Why not let the director get up and perform for you, if you're so lazy as to not even want to answer the most important questions for yourself and then go out and act on them?

Analyze the text. If the need to make a choice arises, make one. Go to rehearsal and present your choices. Don't speak unless spoken to.

Working With a Director

The actor's relationship with the director is very, very simple. The actor does what the director asks. If the director asks you to do something within reason (and practically anything is within reason, except for the obvious things, such as having sex with the director, murder, theft, etc.), you do it. You don't question it. You don't ignore it. You do it. If the director says to you, "You're not emotionally connected to that moment," then you translate that unactable direction into something that's actable and you go out and act on it. Believe me, if a director doesn't like what you're doing or doesn't think what you're doing is going to work, the director will tell you. Perhaps more than any other people in the theater, directors love to hear themselves talk. The director will talk until she loses her voice, if you let her. Much better to keep her quiet, and the way to do this is to not ask questions. Your job isn't to ask questions. Your job is to *do*.

You may think that I'm being unreasonable. I sometimes am, but not when it comes to acting. I've worked with some truly terrible directors. I worked with one director who was so despicable that he emotionally abused the child with whom I was working. The child had very little experience, and thus, didn't understand the tools of the actor. The child needed specialized help. Like far too many adult actors who really have no excuse, the child needed to be spoon-fed the role. But because the director had no understanding of the tools of the actor, the director could only tell the child, in many varied and increasingly insulting ways, that the work he was doing was inadequate. A pretty sight it was not. When this same director would make requests of me, they would consist of requests for "takes" and emotional qualities. Whenever the director would make one of these requests of me, I would nod or say, "Okay" or "All right," translate the unactable direction into something that I could work with and control, and do it. He never gave me a note twice. I never asked any questions. But that was my goal in that particular production: within reason, to do everything that the director asked me to do, no matter how unactable it may have sounded at the time. That was my goal, because I wanted to prove to myself that it could be done. And it could, because that's exactly what I did, and my performance was more than adequate. If it can be done with that truly despicable man, it can be done with anyone.

I'm not saying you should never question the director. Always question authority. But don't waste your time and the director's and the actors' and the designers' and everybody else's with questions that you can answer for yourself. Of course, most questions that you may have you should have answered for yourself before you ever walked through the door for rehearsal, so you shouldn't have to ask that many questions, if any. As I said before, actors should be seen and, except for their lines, not heard.

An Actor Is Not a Director

And while I'm on the subject, don't ever, *ever*, EVER say anything to a fellow actor that could possibly, in any context, in or out of the theater, be construed as direction. A more insulting thing one actor cannot do to another. Don't ever, *ever*, EVER try to place yourself in a position of authority over another actor. How dare you. All actors are equals, no matter the size of the role, no matter the number of lines, no matter the experience, no matter the body of work. The actor does not exist who is better than any or every other actor, and to think anything else is to deny the very nature of what the actor does, to wit: put himself on the line every time he walks onto the stage. Consistently, year after year, the thing people fear the most is not snakes or heights or nuclear war or old age or even death. The thing that people fear the most is *speaking in public*. To assert that your fear is somehow more worthy than another's is a hateful concept.

If there's something you want another actor to do while that actor is onstage with you, get that actor to do it while you're onstage. If you can't figure out a way to make him do what you want him to do while you're onstage with him, either it can't be done, or you just aren't much of an actor anyway.

CHAPTER 26

Blame and Excuses

ONE OF THE MAIN JOBS of an actor is to *adjust*. You'll be required to adjust all the time: to the other actors, to the director, to the set, to your costumes, to the lights, to the audience, to the producer. An actor, every actor, has to adjust all the time. Get used to it. Don't ask others to do it for you. Adjust for them. It's part of your job.

Not only is adjusting part of your job, but if you get into the habit of adjusting, of simply going with the flow as you should be, you'll avoid the blame game. The majority of actors are constantly asked to work in conditions that would be considered less than optimum, usually much less than optimum. I've rehearsed in extreme heat, extreme cold, and in the rain. I once shared rehearsal space with a group of people who were drumming—on actual drums. I've worked in spaces in which the rain falling on the roof and the dogs howling in the next yard were a dramatic part of the performance. I've rehearsed in spaces filled with dust, in attics and in cellars. I've had set pieces fall down onstage during performance, have watched other actors deal with flaming gels, have had people onstage with me forget entire scenes. I've heard about many things much worse than any of these.

Low budget or not, theater is live and real and happening, and often you'll have to deal with the unexpected. You can lose your temper, you can get labeled as a prima donna, you can use people badly and treat them as your servants, or you can simply—*adjust*. Deal with it—preferably with a sense of humor (although I realize that this sometimes isn't possible).

I have often found that less-than-optimum conditions tend to produce effective rehearsals, and sometimes, even lead to effective performances. I can't tell you how many times I've seen actors do their most effective work under bad conditions, and I think it's because they're forced to muster their concentration. I once had a group of actors who went to the first technical rehearsal, which usually occurs a very short time before opening night, with only a sound design—no set, no lights, no costumes. They didn't have the completed set until the day before opening, and they never saw all the light cues until the end of the performance on opening night. (We were doing a light cue-to-cue until fifteen minutes before the house opened, and we didn't have time to finish it). But it ended up being the most effective production of a play, up to that point, that I'd ever had the pleasure of directing, because those actors didn't allow the myriad technical deficits to affect their performances.

Their level of commitment was as high as that of any group of people I've ever worked with. They mustered their concentration and stayed within themselves. And we're not talking about "professionals" here, in the usual sense of that word—we're talking about people with a range of skill and talent. I truly believe that if they'd been run-of-the-mill "professionals," they never would have made it to opening night without either suffering from a major mental or physical illness, or leaving the show. In my admittedly limited experience, "professional" often equates with "spoiled, self-centered brat." If that group of actors can pull off an extremely effective performance under those kinds of conditions, anyone can.

The formula is simple. When you find yourself saying, "It's so difficult to concentrate with all those tech people moving around out there," listen to yourself. You're making an excuse for giving an ineffective performance. What you're really saying is, "I don't want to muster the concentration it will take for me to shut out *all* distractions." Face it. It's not a reason. It's an excuse. You're making an excuse. You're blaming something outside yourself for your own lack of commitment and concentration.

Your performance is always in your hands. Your performance is always your responsibility and yours alone. The tech people aren't responsible for the performance you give. Neither is the director. Neither are the other actors. Neither, ultimately, is the playwright. How many times have we seen an actor giving an effective performance when everyone around him is not? How is it that the one actor managed to take the ineffective script or the ineffective direction and make it effective while the rest did not? Who did his work and who did not? Who played the blame game and who did not?

I'm not saying that there will never be circumstances in which someone does something that's simply wrong or that someone else can never be responsible for some negative occurrence onstage or in the theater. Quite the contrary. Also, I'm not saying that you'll always be able to salvage an ineffective script. But I am saying that, in contemporary society, we've taken to blaming others so often for the state of our lives that it has become habit. No one seems to want to take responsibility for anything. All of us are guilty of it, and if you give in to it regularly, it can only lead you to ineffective acting and deadly theater. Avoid it by becoming aware of the excuses you make as you're making them. *Listen to yourself.* Then, stop making those excuses and take responsibility for what you do. In the theater, you can. Ninety-nine point nine percent of the time. And if you can do it in the theater, you can do it in life, too. I don't know about you, but I think that's a beautiful thing.

CHAPTER 27

Critics

EVERYBODY'S A CRITIC, whether they get paid for it or not. That much I know. I'm one. During my most concentrated period, I watched around two hundred productions over a three-year period and wrote reviews of most of them. I initially went after the job because (1) It paid money, and (2) It was something theatrical that I hadn't done, and I wanted the experience of being a professional audience member. I think there are a lot of other reasons that people take the job. Some take it because there's nobody else who will do it, some because they got a degree in theater and don't know what else to do with it, some because they like wielding power over other people's lives, and being a critic is certainly a way to do that. I think a lot of critics, at one time or another, misuse the power that they're given, misuse it in personal ways that have nothing to do with their actual job.

When I knew I was going to get the position, I wrote a list of rules that I swore to abide by. In each review, without giving too much away, I wanted to tell the story of the play; to describe what I saw and heard; to inform the reader about any material that might be objectionable; and, lastly, to give my opinion about what I saw. I think readers expect critics to be "critical"—to give praise and criticism where and if the critic feels they're due. I especially think that readers expect critics to have strong opinions. Who wants a wimpy critic? If nothing else, the review's entertainment value goes way down.

It was the "opinion" aspect of criticism that got me into trouble, and still gets me into trouble. More than one artistic director went after my head because I had strong opinions and didn't mind expressing them. I don't think I'm stepping too far out of bounds if I say that it's traditional to give a complimentary ticket to a critic who's reviewing a production. In one instance, an artistic director who didn't like some of the reviews I'd written about his theater's productions had one of his minions write to my editor and tell her that, because I was biased and played favorites, I would no longer be given complimentary tickets to his theater's productions; instead, my newspaper would have to pay for my tickets. Fortunately, my employer stood behind me and kept sending me to review every one of that theater's productions for which I was available, paying for each of the tickets. Eventually, the theater dropped the policy.

Dealing With Bias

That charge of bias really got to me because I thought I wasn't biased. I used a set of objective standards to evaluate what I saw, and I could set out those standards at the drop of a hat. Most critics I'm familiar with don't really seem to have any kind of standards that they adhere to, other than personal taste. At the very least, their standards aren't the standards that most people seem to use to evaluate popular entertainment. Some critics seem to want nothing more than to promote their own taste. I believed that I never let my personal taste get in the way. I believed that I was always objective.

I was full of it, at least as far as the charge of bias was concerned. If you know the person taking tickets, you're biased. A theater critic is a member of an arts community, no matter where he lives. Because you're a part of a community, you're going to know, and perhaps even be close to, some, even many, of the members of that community. You're going to want that community to be successful because you're a part of that community. One of the jobs of the critic—perhaps the most important job—is to be able to evaluate what he's seeing while recognizing the biases he has and dealing with them as they present themselves. Just as much as an ability to report on and evaluate what is seen, how well you deal with your biases is what makes you effective or ineffective as a critic.

In the Case of Critics, Ignorance Is Bliss

Biases are there, no denying it. Better not to deny it. Better to recognize that they are. Then you can deal with them. Whenever you as an actor read a review (or listen to a friend or even an audience member talk about your performance), no matter who the critic is, no matter how high or low their station, understand that this particular person is biased in some way about what he's reviewing, and that he's in no way representative of you or any other single individual that makes up the audience for any particular production. This person is representative only of himself. In most cases, the best thing you can do is ignore him altogether. Most critics don't have the slightest clue what they're writing about. For most of them, it really is all a matter of taste. They couldn't recognize their own biases if they tried. Some can, but don't care to deal with them. They even flaunt them. Why shouldn't they? They're above it all. They carry the big sticks. They have no objective standards to work with because they don't care about any standards but their own, and most of them don't even understand what the standards are. All they know is whether or not they like something, and usually, that's all they're going on.

So, the best thing you can do the majority of the time is ignore them. If you don't have the self-discipline to do that, if you just have to know what it is they have to say, or if you actually need them in some way—and yes, there are times when theater people do need critics—then you have to find a way to deal with what they say, good or bad. The best way to do that is to evaluate what they say in the same way that you evaluate what you do and say (at least, I hope you evaluate what you do and say)—religiously and with an iron hand.

Not too long ago, a critic wrote a review of a production that I directed. I knew her personally, so I felt obligated to read her review. (I don't read all reviews of the shows I'm involved in, and I don't read many reviews in general. I usually wait to hear the word of mouth, which is always more reliable than anything any critic has to say.) She had some good things to say and some not-so-good things, but she didn't say anything that I didn't already know, and she said very little that I didn't agree with. I was there the night she saw the show. Of course, I wasn't pleased to see negative things printed for the general public to read about the production, particularly when most of those negative things were about me, but I was objective enough about the production to know that she was, generally speaking, right in what she said. I was also confident that the night she had seen it, the show was not particularly effective, and that there would be better nights. There were. What she had to say didn't affect the show, and it certainly didn't affect the way I behaved after I read the review.

However, reviews can affect you if you let them. I've known actors who would actually change what they were doing because of something a critic wrote. Let's be really clear on this one point: If you change something that you're doing onstage because of something a critic writes or says, you didn't really know what you were doing in the first place. Keep that firmly in your mind. I have yet to read a critical review of a theatrical piece that I thought was totally informed, primarily lacking in bias, and striving for objectivity. I have read reviews that contained one, or even two, of these characteristics, but never one that contained all three. When I do, I will have found a critic in whom I can place my trust, whose advice I will listen to as if it were eternal truth, and whom I will be proud to call my friend. But until I do, I'll read what critics have to say if I have to read it, and then I'll ignore it. You should, too.

CHAPTER 28

The Acting Machine

EVERY ACTOR SHOULD BE AN ACTING MACHINE.

People have told me that I want to be another Gordon Craig, with the *über*-marionettes and such. I don't. There's no way that I want to lose the human element. It makes live theater exactly that—live. Marionettes aren't live. Marionettes are puppets, wood and cloth and strings. Not what I want at all. I want an actor who can *feel* a rhythm. Can *feel* a pause. Can *feel* when the tempo is right. Can *feel* when a scene is working. I don't want an actor who can actually run the scene the same way every time, who can go on autopilot and give me a bloodless rendition of whatever plan she's formed. I want an actor who is *striving* to do the scene the same way every time, not one who can. I want one who's *really* listening, one who's really trying to *get* something from that other person, one who's going to be able to recognize something new *as it happens* and then allow herself to go with the flow and *let it happen*. That's not a puppet. That's a full, flesh-and-blood, *human* being.

So just what do I mean when I say that every actor should be an acting machine?

What I mean is that every actor should understand all the tools of the craft and have the ability to manipulate those tools at will, that every actor should be willing to work harder than anyone else who is working on a production, giving 100 percent of herself to the process. I'm not saying that every actor will be able to do everything that it is possible for every human being to do. We're all limited by who we are. We can't all hit a high "C." But within those certain limitations, every actor should be able to manipulate the tools at her disposal.

Of course, that's only if you're approaching acting as a craft and not as an exercise in ego. And that's the very few. The very, very few. Most approach it strictly as a "look at me" kind of thing. I directed an actor once who had been singing since she was a very small child. She sang with her mother, but she swore up and down that she didn't sing because she enjoyed the attention from her mother or anyone else. This doesn't make logical sense to me. I've had babies. I've watched them grow. I know how they operate. When they first learn to smile, babies—little ones—may do it instinctually, but eventually they smile a lot because it has an effect on the people who are watching them. They do it because it gets a positive reaction. They don't do it because they want to learn the "craft of smiling." They do it because it gets them a certain kind of attention.

And yes, you can act for that reason. You can also act for money (although that's pretty foolish, for obvious reasons). But I think these are lousy reasons to act. I think these are lousy reasons to practice any art or craft. You should act because you want to work on your self. You should act because you want to learn about your self. You should act because you want to learn about the human condition. You should act because, like the carpenter, the architect, and the glassblower, you want to learn a craft. You want to be a craftsman. You want to construct a well-built house.

Sure, you can concentrate on what's outside of you. If you like, you can focus strictly on the things of this world. But to what end? You think you'll find what you're looking for there? If that were the case, why does any actor who has ever had a successful run keep acting? *It isn't out there. What you're looking for isn't out there.*

It's in you. Inside you. All you're looking for is already in you. In the end, you are all you have. In the end, we all die alone. Best to know ourselves. Best to seek our own approval than to seek the approval of others. Best to be whole alone than scattered in a crowd.

Are you ready?

Then let's *begin.*

An Outline of a Technique for Effective Acting

A. Three Prerequisites

1. **A mind within the range of normal.** If you don't have a mind that's psychologically within the range of normal, then chances are you'll have great difficulty mastering the technique outlined herein.
2. **A loud, clear voice.** If you don't have a loud, clear voice, start working on obtaining one. It's easier to obtain a loud, clear voice than to obtain prerequisite #1, above, or prerequisite #3, below.
3. **The ability to memorize sequences of words.** You have to learn how to do this on your own. But, believe it or not, you have to learn to do *all* of this stuff pretty much on your own, and like anything else, the longer you do it, the easier it becomes.

B. The Tools

1. **Analysis**—the breaking down into parts. Because every story has parts, every story is subject to analysis. Plays are stories. Therefore, plays are subject to analysis. What follows immediately below are the tools you utilize when analyzing a play:
   a. **Beats**—a little part of a story and an actor's most basic unit of analysis. Beats have beginnings and endings, and

the ending of one beat and beginning of the next is referred to as a "beat change." When looking for a beat change, look for:

(i) A complete line of thought (by far the most important indicator of a beat)

(ii) Repetition of words, phrases, and/or ideas [not nearly as important as (i)].

When scoring (marking with a pencil) a text for beats, indicate the end of one beat and the beginning of the next by using a slash mark ("/"). Any given text will have only one possible set of beats.

b. **Key phrases**. The most important phrases in any given text, key phrases consist of groups of two or more words. While key phrases are found in the middles and at the ends of beats, most consistently they are found at the beginnings of beats, and almost invariably, no matter where they're located within a beat, they'll focus on necessary information concerning the story you're telling. When scoring a text for key phrases, circle them. In any given text, 35 to 40 percent of the words will be circled.

c. **Key words**. Single words that receive the most stress in any given group of words. Key words are used in conjunction with key phrases to put across the sense of the story you're telling. When scoring a text for key words, underline them. In any given text, on average, one of eight words will be keyed. Do not underline—key—two consecutive words unless they're separated by some form of punctuation that acts as a caesura. Only a *single* word can be a key word. If you're tempted to underline two words in a row, then you have a key phrase, not a key word, and you should circle the phrase. Key phrases may contain key words, but key words are found throughout a text, not only in key phrases.

d. **Story**. You should be able to tell the story of any given beat using the following as a form: "This beat is about _____." You should be able to fill in the blank with eight words or less, using the language of the play as much as possible to fill in the blank. If you feel compelled to use more than eight words to describe any given beat, then you most likely haven't marked the beats correctly.

e. **Action**. You should be able to state the action of your character in each beat (**beat actions**), as well as the action of your character for the play as a whole (**main action**). Any action should be written in the form: "to _____." Because you want any main or beat action statement to be as simple, and thus as easily remembered, as possible, fill in the blank with a transitive verb, preferably one that (1) takes a human object and (2) implies a strong set of physical and vocal tactics. In addition to the transitive verb, you also may wish to fill in the blank with an object for the verb. However, this isn't required, as the vast majority of the time, the object of your action will be the person(s) you're speaking to.

2. **Presentation**. Delivering text to an audience. Any given actor will act effectively if she understands how to apply the tools of analysis to a text and how to apply the tools of presentation to an analysis. What follows immediately below are the tools you utilize in presenting your analysis:

a. **Tempo**—How quickly or slowly you say something. If something in your text is circled (a key phrase), then chances are you'll say it more slowly than something that isn't circled. Commonly, tempo will build (increase) through the middle of a beat, reaching its high point (climax) toward the end of a beat.

b. **Volume**—How loudly or softly you say something. Often, volume, along with tempo, will build the closer you get to the end of a beat. More than occasionally, the last line or phrase of a beat will receive the most volume in the beat. Also, the most common way to key (stress) a word is by increasing its volume relative to the overall volume that has been established at any given point in a beat.

c. **Intensity**—Strength, energy, force. Not to be confused with volume; e.g., while the most common way to key a word is by increasing its volume, you may key a word simply by adding intensity. Intensity will sometimes build the closer you get to the end of a beat. [NOTE: *The three tools above are the most powerful vocal tools at the actor's disposal.*]

d. **Movement**—The process of changing physical position. The text and your analysis of it dictate all choices concerning movement, and all movement should support the text and occur on the rhythm of the text. This includes elements that are extra-textual and contain a rhythm, such as music and changing lights. Put as simply as possible, you shouldn't move any part of your instrument (body) except those parts that are needed to present the text effectively.

e. **Focus**—Where you look when you're on the stage. Like all the other tools mentioned above, where and when you focus should be dictated by the text and your analysis of it, and all focus changes should support the text and occur on the rhythm of the text. Like speaking and gesture, focus is a specific kind of movement, and probably the most ignored of an actor's presentational tools. People and elements not present on the stage can be made present by the effective manipulation of focus.

f. **Stillness**—The cessation of movement. *All* movement. In almost every instance, all movement should cease—stillness should occur, if only for the slightest moment—at a beat change.

g. **Rhythm**—An ordered, recurrent alternation of strong and weak elements in the flow of sound and silence in speech and the physical flow of movement, including the grouping of weaker elements around stronger, the distribution and relative disposition of strong and weak elements, and the general quantitative relations of these elements and their combinations. This tool is dictated entirely by the form of the text—by the words themselves, where beats change, by key phrases and key words, by caesuras (pauses, long pauses, silences, and any other indications of the cessation of sound and/or movement), by punctuation, and by extra-textual elements that contain a rhythm, such as music and changing lights.

h. **Pitch and Resonance**—Two very specific, very specialized vocal tools, neither of which is addressed to any great extent in this book. Pitch is the highness or lowness of sound. Often, a voice that is pitched too high can be irritating to listen to, and so should be avoided. Resonance is the deepening and/or enriching of sound. It is a powerful, but extremely specialized and specific, vocal tool.

3. **Activation.** Allowing a story to live (by far the most difficult thing to achieve in acting).

a. **Playing Your Action**—concentrating on your main action (the transitive verb you've chosen for the play as a whole) at any given moment. Beat actions are used as analytical tools, and if you've chosen verbs for your beat actions that take human objects and imply strong sets of physical and vocal tactics, then you may use them as you rehearse to help you change your tactics at a beat change. An example I'm fond of using: "Seducing" someone is very different from "flirting" with someone. "Seduce" implies one set of physical and vocal tactics and "flirt" implies a completely different set, yet both come from a similar need—to interact sexually. In life, whether consciously or not, we always are playing an action. We walk into any given room with a plan, and we take action to get the things we want. The latter statement, of course, implies an objective—a need, want, or desire on the part of the actor—but discussing actions and objectives is like discussing chickens and eggs. Needs, wants, and desires are often easily understood and articulated. Actions are not—but it is our actions that define us most clearly and make us what we are.

b. **Listening.** Paying attention to what another person is saying. This is the most difficult thing any actor is required to do, even more difficult than playing an action. When I say that an actor needs to listen onstage, I mean an actor needs to listen the same way an actor listens in life. In life, we listen in order to interact. In the theater, most actors, perhaps all actors, listen only for their cue, which will enable them to say their next line. Most actors listen to "react," and thus end up making faces or doing physical things to "indicate" that listening is occurring, but in life, we listen *to interact*. Almost everything we do in life, including listening, is done with a purpose directed at another person in order to interact, and the theater should be no different. Playing your action and learning to listen are exceedingly difficult, but if each can be achieved, then the theater and life become one. The theater becomes life in its truest, richest sense.

C. The Two Hard-and-Fast Rules of Acting

1. **If everything weighs the same, everything weighs nothing**. The analytical and presentational tools outlined above proceed directly from this very simple truth.

2. **Emotion is not an acting tool.** A tool is something you can control. To a great extent, you can control each of the analytical and presentational tools outlined above. Controlling your emotions is a physical and intellectual impossibility. Since you can't control your emotions, it logically follows that emotions aren't a tool. Emotions are a product, for both the actor and the audience. If emotions aren't a tool, then why include this rule? Because most modern acting theory, in one way or another, centers on emotion, and if you accept that emotions aren't a tool, it follows that the bulk of modern acting theory is, practically speaking, useless.

A Sample Monologue Score

Please note that in the script below, beats are marked with a slash mark ("/"), key phrases are bolded rather than circled, and key words are underlined.

From William Shakespeare's MACBETH

Main action: **to control my fears**

To be thus is nothing;	to intrigue (the audience)
But to be safely thus./	
Our fears in Banquo stick deep,	to alert (the audience)
And in his royalty of nature reigns that	
Which would be fear'd. **'Tis much he dares,**	
And to that dauntless temper of his mind,	
He hath a wisdom that doth guide his valor	
To act in safety. **There is none but he**	
Whose being I do fear, and under him	
My genius is rebuk'd, as it is said	
Marc Antony's was by Caesar./	
He chid the sisters	to ignite (the audience)
When first they put the name of king upon me,	
And bade them speak to him. Then prophet-like	
They hail'd him father to a line of kings.	

Upon my <u>head</u> they plac'd a <u>fruitless</u> crown,
And put a <u>barren</u> scepter in my grip,
Thence to be wrench'd with an unlineal hand,
No <u>son</u> of mine succeeding./
If 't be so,   to impassion (the audience)
For Banquo's issue have I <u>'fil'd</u> my mind;
For them the gracious Duncan have I <u>murder'd</u>,
Put rancors in the vessel of my peace
Only for <u>them</u>. **And mine eternal <u>jewel</u>**
Given to the common <u>enemy</u> of man,
To make them <u>kings</u>,
the seeds of Banquo kings!/
Rather than so, **come, <u>fate</u>**, into the list   to invoke (the fates)
And champion me to the <u>utterance</u>!

Note how each of the actions above is a transitive verb that implies a strong set of physical and vocal tactics. Also note how each of the beat actions builds on the previous one, even though it isn't always possible to have them do so. Finally, with one exception, each of the verbs takes a human object. (I take a mulligan on "the fates," as I'm certain that Macbeth thinks of them as human too.) I include the objects of the beat actions in a purely informational sense. I think they're obvious.

Story

Note how each beat description is a paraphrase of what's said by Macbeth in any given beat, using, as much as possible, the language of the play:

- The first beat is about being safe as king.
- The second beat is about my fear of Banquo.
- The third beat is about what the witches said concerning Banquo and me.
- The fourth beat is about the fate I may have brought upon myself.
- The fifth beat is about making fate my champion.

Here is the statistical breakdown of key phrases and key words for the monologue:

- Two hundred and four words in the monologue. Eighty-four bolded (circled). That's 41 percent of the words in the monologue, within acceptable limits to the optimal 35 to 40 percent.
- Twenty-nine words underlined (keyed). That's one of seven words keyed, which is within acceptable limits to the optimal one of eight.

Additional Analytical Notes

Note that the key phrases as a whole read like the monologue in miniature, delivering the "story" of the monologue. Also, note that, with one exception, every phrase that begins a beat has been bolded (circled) out of necessity because every one of them is important to the "story" of the monologue. In three out of five instances, the phrase that ends a beat is also circled, and again from necessity: The first two ("But to be safely thus"; "no son of mine succeeding") deliver plot (story) information, and the last ("the seeds of Banquo kings") is the ultimate climax, or highest point, in the monologue. All this bolding (circling) of phrases and keying of words fall into line with the idea that a beat has "exposition" and "building action." That is, you take time with what's most important (exposition) and drive the tempo (building action) to the climax, which will come toward the end of a beat (or monologue, scene, act, play).

Now, you can nitpick me on my key words if you like (as my workshop participants know, I rarely hesitate to nitpick them), but I chose them with great care and, like the key phrases, the key words tell the story of the speech in miniature. Also note how the keys I've chosen follow what I've outlined as the story of the beat: "safely" is keyed in the first beat; "fears" is keyed in the second; "father," "line," "fruitless," and "barren" in the third; "If 't" in the fourth; and "come" in the fifth.

Presentational Notes

Now read it out loud, keeping in mind the following:

1. If it's bolded (circled), use a relatively slow tempo.
2. When you come to a beat change, go still (cease all movement), if only for the briefest of moments, then begin to deliver the next beat.
3. When you come to a phrase that is not bolded (circled), begin to push (drive) the tempo. Not too much initially, but just enough so that there's a difference between what you've slowed and what you now drive. The further you move into a beat, the more you push (drive) the tempo.
4. When you come to a key word, stress it by giving it more volume (as I just stressed "stress" by using italics). Increasing its volume is the easiest way to vocally emphasize a key word. I have italics. You have volume.

After you've read it aloud that way a few times, try adding another element: building the beats to a climax. That is, increase the tempo and volume the further you go in the beat, pulling back in a relative fashion as you encounter key phrases, and then picking up where you left off and building again. Though it is a more specialized use of the tools, the ability to allow the dialogue to ebb and flow is essential to effective acting.

Also keep in mind that dialogue, almost without exception, always builds—that is, the overall tempo will always increase, if only ever so slightly, the further you move into a beat. (I'd go so far as to postulate that audiences get bored watching plays partially because actors far too often use the same tempo as they deliver text in any given beat. In other words, they don't build their beats effectively. The tempo in any beat should almost always increase, if only ever so slightly, keeping in mind that it will ebb and flow in accordance with what you've chosen as key phrases.)

What follows here are where I see the "climaxes," or "highest points," of each individual beat (note that each of the single words is keyed in the score):

- Beat 1: Climaxes on the word "safely."
- Beat 2: Climaxes on the word "rebuk'd."

- Beat 3: Climaxes on the word "barren."
- Beat 4: Climaxes on the phrase "the seeds of Banquo kings."
- Beat 5: Climaxes on the word "utterance."

As for building action, three of the beats are somewhat specialized, in that information in the middle of a beat is bolded (circled). As you come to each of these, pull back slightly on the tempo and the volume and, once you've gotten through the bolded (circled) material, pick up where you left off, pushing (driving) and increasing the tempo and volume again as you build toward the climax.

After you've read it aloud a few more times with these additional elements in mind, go back to the chapter on "Focus" and attempt to add in the focus changes I suggest for the monologue.

I haven't, to this point, suggested hand gestures for the monologue, but I believe that only one is absolutely necessary: Assuming you've stood with your hands in a relaxed position at your sides as you've delivered the text, in the last beat, as you say the word "come," sharply turn your hands, palm outward, slightly away from your body. This will help underline the idea that Macbeth is "invoking" fate. Otherwise, the only movement I would utilize is the movement of your head as you change focal points, and the movement of your vocal instrument as you deliver the lines. Keep in mind that I'm not saying other gestures won't work—on the contrary, I think this soliloquy can work with more than a few gestures. All I'm saying is that they aren't necessary. The soliloquy can work with just the one.

In Conclusion

While it may be an impossibility to direct through the written word, given that limitation, I didn't want to leave you without as concrete an example of the technique as I could offer. What I've done above is attempt to allow you to practice the technique on your own with a specific piece of text. Any other text—*every* other text—works exactly the same way. Every other text lends itself to scoring, and the use of the presentational tools follows the pattern of the score. Because you're a born storyteller, if you follow the instructions I've given above, I have little doubt that you'll be able to deliver this monologue from *Macbeth* in an effective manner. Will it be great acting? Probably not. But as I've said previously, great acting is a function of actor, role, director, time, place, and myriad other elements that are totally beyond the individual actor's control. Besides, great acting isn't what we should be looking for. Just acting that's true to the play. Just acting that works.

A Sample Scene Score

What follows here is a scene from Monika Bustamante's play entitled *Perdita*. The scoring work isn't mine, but was done by a participant in my workshop, Parker-Williams. You'll find the comments I offered to Parker at the end of the score.

As you review the score, note that Parker scores only for the character she presents, Marnie, and not for the character of Goldie, with one exception: Parker scores *all* the beats. Scoring all the beats in a scene is necessary so that you'll know when you should be still and when you can move. When you score a scene, you should score *all* the beats, but only the key phrases, key words, and actions for your individual character, as Parker does in this scene.

As with the monologue score in appendix B, Parker has bolded, rather than circled, key phrases. Also, she has conveniently written numbers at the beginnings of her beats. Normally, of course, an actor wouldn't mark the first beat or use numbers, but she has done so here for clarity's sake and for ease of use.

Although you won't find them in this scene, which speaks directly to Ms. Bustamante's good sense as a playwright, you'll often find playwrights who offer a few words (eagerly, fearful, etc.), usually parenthetically, throughout the course of a play that indicate emotions and states of being. Some playwrights think of themselves as the ultimate directors, but in any script, you should mark through—preferably in a dark, indelible ink—any words that indicate emotions, attitudes, or states of being, because *they are not playable*.

Lastly, as you review this score, keep in mind that I had more than a few problems with what Parker marked as the beat changes. As you read, keep a mental ear out for the places where the story turns corners, and thus, changes a beat. If you're sharp, you'll find more than a few beat changes that Parker missed. (And many thanks to Parker for being such an excellent example for us all.)

Scene Score from Monika Bustamante's "Perdita"

Main action: **contain**

MARNIE: EMBRACE 1/ Good **morning, sunshine!**

GOLDIE: You're being too loud.

MARNIE: I'm <u>sorry</u>.

GOLDIE: Don't be sorry; be quiet, Christ. Don't open the curtains yet.

MARNIE: Okay.

GOLDIE: CORNER 2/ What time is it?

MARNIE: Early.

GOLDIE: Are the neighbors home yet?

MARNIE: Home from <u>where</u>?

GOLDIE: They went out in the middle of the night. I saw their headlights on the wall. Haven't heard 'em come back, 'cept maybe I drifted off.

MARNIE: **You've been awake, <u>waiting</u>** for them to come home?

GOLDIE: Wasn't hard. Don't need much sleep. They home?

MARNIE peeks through a crack in the curtain.

MARNIE: OCCUPY 3/ **Do they keep the car in the <u>garage</u>?**

GOLDIE: How the hell do I know?

MARNIE: Seems like something <u>you</u> would know.

GOLDIE: Yeah, I suppose they do. Damn.

MARNIE: What do you <u>care</u> what they do?

GOLDIE: Don't trust 'em. Highly suspicious. Husband's off his rocker, wife's even worse.

MARNIE: Oh, yeah? What are they u̲p to?

GOLDIE: I have my theories. I know when someone's caught up in something not-right. I know if someone's doing dark things. It's a smell.

ENCOURAGE 4/ Smell is the last sense to go. Some people say it's hearing, but it's smell, rest assured. I could tell that last girl who worked here was coming up the walk every time cause I'd smell that old White Shoulders. Most disgusting sweet smell, that perfume.

MARNIE: What about m̲e̲?

GOLDIE: *She sniffs.* Old lady and pee. I'm assuming that's my fault. That's not entirely true, though, your hair smells real nice. Honey, I think.

MARNIE: My s̲h̲a̲m̲p̲o̲o̲.

GOLDIE: It's nice. Reminds me of Cecile.

ENGAGE 5/ I dreamed about her last night.

MARNIE: **I thought you didn't s̲l̲e̲e̲p̲**.

GOLDIE: Don't be argumentative. I'm sharing something with you.

MARNIE: Sorry.

GOLDIE: We were ice fishing. Up in Canada, I think. It was just like in the cartoons—we had a perfect circle cut in the middle of a lake, and lawn chairs set up around it. We were wearing fur coats and sunglasses, and Cecile had one of those fur muffs to keep her hands warm.

MARNIE: Did you c̲a̲t̲c̲h̲ anything?

GOLDIE: I felt my line tug, but it snapped. Then, whatever it was took Cecile's line and she leapt out of her chair and jumped right in the hole after it. Fur and all. She always knew what she wanted. The night we met she took my arm and said, "You. I'm going with you." I woke myself up trying to go in after her. Thirty some-odd years together, and she's still got me chasing her.

MARNIE: MAINTAIN 6/ **Time for your m̲e̲d̲i̲c̲i̲n̲e̲**.

GOLDIE: Does this story make you uncomfortable?

MARNIE: Not at all.

GOLDIE: Can't figure out how someone could love an old crab like me, is that it?

MARNIE: Of <u>course</u> not.

GOLDIE: You keep so quiet, you act so smug. Everyone deserves love, you know. It's not only for the young.

MARNIE: I know that. I <u>know</u> that.

GOLDIE: I was your age once. Think about that.

MARNIE: APPEASE 7/ **Can I open the <u>curtains</u>** now?

GOLDIE: Yeah, go ahead.

MARNIE: *(as she opens them)* We should <u>dust</u> in here. **It's hard to breathe.**

GOLDIE: *(after a moment, apologetically)*
CONSIDER 8/ Does the agency pay you well?

MARNIE: It's fine for now. I get <u>health</u> insurance; **it works with my school schedule.** You know.

MARNIE begins to remove pills from various bottles on a nightstand.

GOLDIE: ASSAUGE 9/ You've got tired eyes today. You up late studying?

MARNIE: **I couldn't sleep.** I <u>tossed</u> and turned. Then I started writing in my <u>journal</u> and couldn't stop.

GOLDIE: Poetry?

MARNIE: Just a way of <u>remembering</u> things. **But I do have an exam** today.

GOLDIE: *(trying to remember)* What are you studying? Bugs?

MARNIE: <u>Butterflies</u>, mostly, and moths.

GOLDIE: What's the point?

MARNIE: Well . . . I just find it <u>interesting</u>.

GOLDIE: Can you make money doing that?

MARNIE: Some <u>people</u> do.

GOLDIE: As much as taking care of an old lady?

MARNIE: Probably <u>more</u>.

GOLDIE: Huh.

INSPIRE 10/ Where would you get a job like that?

MARNIE: I'm not sure yet. **I had an internship last summer. Nicaragua.** A nature preserve. Maybe something like that.

GOLDIE: Nicaragua? You couldn't pay me to go to Nicaragua.

MARNIE: It was <u>beautiful</u>.

GOLDIE: Like how?

MARNIE: **So many trees**, not like any I've ever seen here, but giants of trees with enormous vines, and **so many amazing insects.** Everything is dark and green.

GOLDIE: I've heard it's full of criminals. Did you get held up?

MARNIE: No. Some people in my program did. Their cameras were stolen, and their shoes.

GOLDIE: Uh-huh. Hardly seems worth it just to look at some bugs. INCLUDE II/ How'd you get interested in that, anyway?

MARNIE: **My father's church in one of the towns where I grew up,** it was around the corner from the science - museum. **My brother and I would sneak over there during his sermons.** There was an interactive part, where there were bugs to touch and buttons to push so you could hear the sounds they made. **But the best was this atrium you could walk through,** walls of glass, a waterfall. And in there were the most beautiful butterflies, from Brazil and Africa, Colombia and Japan, and they would flutter around and land on you. **On the way out, there was a life cycle display,** and you could see them in all their stages of development, from larvae to caterpillar to cocoon to butterfly. **The mosque for the cocoons was my favorite.** It was very dark, and it had the strangest smell. Musky, and warm.

GOLDIE: Gross.

MARNIE: Yeah, I loved it. **We spent hours in there, until he caught us.**

> *She jingles the pills in her hand.*

PACIFY I2/ Okay, swallowing time. **What do you want to drink?**

GOLDIE: Scotch.

> *MARNIE doesn't move.*

Okay, orange juice.

> *MARNIE goes out, comes back with juice. She returns to GOLDIE.*

MARNIE: Drink up, buttercup.

GOLDIE: What are all my pills for?

MARNIE: **Haven't we been over this?**

GOLDIE: Well, I can't remember, that's what it's like when you get to be my age. You're working on being wise, and meanwhile you can't remember where you've left your teeth.

MARNIE: Okay, <u>okay</u>, here we go.

> *She holds up a bottle to illustrate each of their uses.*
> *GOLDIE swallows the pills one at a time as they are listed off.*

MARNIE: <u>These</u> are for your blood pressure—**you don't have <u>high</u> blood pressure, but they think that blood pressure medications may help your <u>kidneys</u> function a little better.**

GOLDIE: Who says?

MARNIE: The <u>agency</u>. These *(She holds up another bottle)* **are your <u>insulin</u> pills.**

GOLDIE: You take that, too.

MARNIE: Right. **But my <u>pancreas</u> doesn't work at all, and I have to take <u>shots</u> for it.**

GOLDIE: And I just ate too much.

MARNIE: Something like that. *(Another bottle)* **These are for your cholesterol**, which <u>is</u> a little high.

GOLDIE: Which ones are those? The blue ones?

MARNIE: *(Looking in bottle)* Yep, blue. And these *(Another bottle)* are for <u>incontinence</u>.

GOLDIE: I shouldn't be taking those. I'm already wearing diapers, what's the point?

MARNIE: Tell your <u>doctor</u>. *(Another bottle)* **These are an antibiotic to ward off <u>infections</u>** since your immune system is <u>weakened</u>. *(Another bottle)* These are your multivitamins.

GOLDIE: Horse pill.

MARNIE: Yes. *(Another bottle)* **These are for <u>depression</u>,** they're the ones you only take <u>once</u> a day. *(Another bottle)* These are for your <u>pain</u>, for your hip. *(Another bottle)* This is your thyroid medication. *(Another bottle)* These are the <u>feel-good</u> ones. *(Last bottle)* **And these are to help you <u>sleep</u>.**

GOLDIE: HOLD 13/ You know what would happen if I stopped taking all of them?

MARNIE: You wouldn't do that.

GOLDIE: Me? No. I want to finish myself off, I'll come up with a quicker way than that—it isn't pretty. That last *girl* decided she'd had enough of me, but didn't tell the agency she wasn't coming back. She didn't leave the phone near, and the agency missed their check-in call, so by the time they finally came over, all sorts of hell had broken loose.

MARNIE: Did you have to go to the <u>hospital</u>?

GOLDIE: Two weeks. And I needed a new mattress, that's for sure. But I didn't have to pay for it.

(A pause.)

EMBRACE 14/ I hate this bed. I'm sick of sleeping. I don't like to dream.

MARNIE: Me <u>either</u>.

GOLDIE: Why not you?

MARNIE: **I dream about things I don't want to <u>think</u> about when I'm awake.**

GOLDIE: I dream about everything I've lost. And it's hell.

> *A noise from outside. MARNIE goes to the window.*

GOLDIE: INVOLVE 15/ What is it, is it them?

MARNIE: They just <u>pulled</u> up.

GOLDIE: What do they look like? Are they acting funny? Don't let them see you now, stay near the curtain.

MARNIE: **They're not <u>looking</u> this way.** They're <u>getting</u> groceries out of the car. Hang on, **I'm going to go look from the window in the <u>bathroom</u>.**

> *She goes offstage.*

I can see better in here, **the <u>tree</u> isn't in the way.**

GOLDIE: I need to trim that tree.

MARNIE: **Are you <u>sure</u> they didn't come home all night?**

GOLDIE: I hear everything.

MARNIE: Well, not that I know what this <u>means</u>, **but they're kind of . . .**

GOLDIE: What?

MARNIE: Dirty.

Comments

Following are the comments I offered to Parker on the score. Pay close to attention to what I've written regarding the beats, and see if you don't agree. You will, of course, have to go back and compare what Parker has marked as her beats to what I suggest she should have marked, but this acting stuff always requires more than a bit of work, doesn't it?

Dear Parker:

Beats

I think there's a beat change at "they do. Damn/What do you."

I think there's a beat change at "that's my fault/That's not entirely."

I think there's a beat change at "Fur and all/She always knew."

Definitely a beat change at "find it interesting/Can you make."

I think there's a beat change at "dark and green/I've heard it's."

Definitely a beat change at "Okay, orange juice/Drink up, buttercup." The playwright even has you making a large physical movement at the beat change.

I think there's a beat change at "here we go/These are for" as well.

There's a beat change at almost every mention of a new pill. The dead giveaway on that is that you've circled the phrase at the beginning of almost every "pill" beat. Here's where I see 'em:

The agency/These are yours

Something like that/These are for

Yep, blue/And these are

Tell your doctor/These are an

That last one is an exception—it's the beat about "the rest of the pills." Another dead giveaway is the fact that, when you performed the scene, you made a relatively large physical movement at the beginning of each of those beats (as I recall), with the exception of the last one, where you didn't pick up each individual bottle. Did I get that right? In other words, your instincts (or conscious choices) about the beat changes were right on—you just didn't mark the beats.

Definitely a beat change at "of the car/Hang on, I'm."

Phrases

Very nice work with these.

I'd circle "What do you care" in "What do you care what they do?"

I'd circle "What are they up to?"

I'd definitely circle "the most beautiful butterflies."

I'd definitely circle "They just pulled up."

Key Words

I love the way you'll use a key word to put across plot-centered information when you're not circling a phrase at the beginning of a beat. That's perfect. I mean, why circle something when just keying a word will do?

Please forgive my nitpickiness. I'm in a nitpicky mood.

Not so sure you need to key "sorry" in "I'm sorry."

I'd key "would" instead of "you" in "Seems like something you would know." (Watch out for keying those pronouns. But it works when you key "me" in "What about me?")

I don't think I'd key "interesting" in "I just find it interesting."

I'd key "Some" instead of "people" in "Some people do."

I think keying "grew" in "the towns where I grew up" is awkward. It even looks awkward on the page. Otherwise, you've keyed that little monologue nicely.

I find the choice of keying "is" in "which is a little high" interesting. My choice probably would have been "cholesterol," but I can go with "is."

Don't key both "feel" and "good"—just one. I'd choose "feel."

Keying "pulled" in "They just pulled up" is awkward. If I'm going to key something in that line, it's going to be "up."

I'd key "groceries" instead of "getting" in "They're getting groceries out of the car."

Actions

Main: When I first looked at "contain," I went, "Huh?" But after looking up the definition, I get it. And it wouldn't surprise me if it worked for the entire play.

Beats: First, a note. Despite the fact that I really believe there's a beat change at all the places I've noted concerning the pills, I don't think the action necessarily changes at each of the beat changes. I know that sounds radical, as we often discuss the fact that what changes at a beat change are the actions of the characters. However, there is an exception to every rule (except, of course, to the "if everything weighs the same, everything weighs nothing" rule and the "emotion is not a tool" rule). As for the beats about the individual pills, I think we have an exception—one of the few I've run into *ever*. Also, just as a side note: While I think Marnie's action remains basically the same for each of those beats (there may be one or two exceptions), Goldie's action, I believe, changes more often than not. That said—

I don't think "corner" works in what you've got marked as the second beat. I can see it for some of the beat, but can't in the rest. I do, however, like the contrast between the action for the first beat and the action for the second. Shows how you are forced to adjust because of the action of the other character.

I love where you've used "appease." I think that's very effective. A very nice choice.

I'll go for "consider," but I have my doubts.

I also like "inspire" quite a bit. Another very nice choice.

I'd never looked up the definition for "hold" before. I know because when I saw how many definitions there are,

I about freaked. Given the number of transitive uses for "hold," I'm surprised no one has ever used it before. It's a nice, tension-filled verb, when you consider.

You repeated yourself! In what you have marked as beat 14, you used "embrace," just like in beat 1! No, no, no.

That's it!

Love,

Barry

Other Stuff You Should Read

What follows below is a list of the things I've read that have had the greatest impact on my life, both inside the theater and outside.

Anything by Derrick Jensen, but most especially *A Language Older than Words* and *The Culture of Make-Believe* (Thank you for being who you are, Derrick.)

Daniel Quinn's *Ishmael*

Don Miguel Ruiz's *The Four Agreements*

Charlotte Brontë's *Jane Eyre*

Anything by William Shakespeare, but most especially *Hamlet*, *King Lear*, *Macbeth*, *Othello*, *Julius Caesar*, *Titus Andronicus*, *Romeo and Juliet*, *A Midsummer Night's Dream*, *The Merchant of Venice*, *The Taming of the Shrew*, *The Tempest*, *Twelfth Night*, *Henry V*, and *Richard III*

David Mamet's *American Buffalo* and *True and False: Heresy and Common Sense for the Actor* (the most valuable book on the craft of acting in existence)

Konstantin Stanislavsky's *An Actor Prepares*

Tennessee Williams's *The Glass Menagerie*

Arthur Miller's *The Crucible*, *Death of a Salesman*, and *All My Sons*

Eugene O'Neill's *The Hairy Ape*, *Anna Christie*, and *Long Day's Journey Into Night*

Samuel Beckett's *Waiting for Godot*

Harold Pinter's *The Birthday Party*

Edward Albee's *The Zoo Story*
Sam Shepard's *Buried Child*
Mark Ravenhill's *Shopping and Fucking*
Sarah Kane's *Cleansed*
Walt Whitman's *Song of Myself*

And, if you will indulge me one moment longer, allow me also to recommend a magazine: *The Sun*, a magazine about what being human means and the only magazine I know of to be vaguely worth the trees upon which it is printed.

Acknowledgments

Nothing in life is done without help of some kind. *Absolutely* nothing, and so it is with this text. My wife, Johanna Whitmore, and I have probably spent more hours discussing acting and theater than we have doing anything else but working and sleeping. I wouldn't have written a single word without her influence, care, and love.

I've learned far more because of my workshop participants, past and present, than any one of them ever has because of me. As of this writing, they are: Heather Barfield, Elizabeth Doss, Amie Elyn, Steven Fay, Courtney Hopkin, Ellen Kolstö, David McDaniel, John Steven Rodriguez, and Stephanie Towery (the original nine); Jim Arnold, Michael Beckham, Maggie Bell, Beth Burroughs, Teresa Castle, Blythe Day, Randa Downs, Todd Essary, P.J. Evans, Nicole Furneisen, Paula Gilbert, Juliana Gilchrist, Charles Hobby, Traci Laird, James "Woodstock" Laljer, Taylor Maddux, Gareth Maguire, Marilyn McConnell, Gwen McLendon, Brandon Nagle, Ryan Nagle, Dave Pantano, Matthew Patterson, Martinique Duchene Phillips, Weldon Phillips, Rhonda Raymond, Tina Reppenhagen, Ash Robinson, Catherine Rose, David Saldaña, Samantha Scott, Jericho Thorp, Ryan Voight, and last (but certainly, certainly never least), Parker-Williams. I most especially thank Stephanie Towery for being my friend as well as my most valued colleague. Her influence on this book is immeasurable.

I'm especially grateful for all the directors over the years (even the ineffective and the just plain bad ones) who gave me the opportunity to practice the craft, but particularly for Sumner Hayward, who cast a lonely fourteen-year-old in his first play and gave him a ton of lines and had him freeze onstage for a full five minutes, long before he ever had to say a word, with nervous sweat pouring in streams down the insides of his arms; for Elizabeth Merrill, who taught that same young man the three most important rules of acting—face the audience, speak loudly and clearly, and don't break character or you will pay dearly; and for Robin Lisherness and Tom Whitaker, not only for what they helped me learn, but simply for being who they were, which is much more difficult for any individual than anyone might imagine.

I also am especially grateful for James A. Bannerot, one of the finest human beings I've ever met, who gainfully employed me for many years in a job he knew I despised, and who turned a blind eye to the theatrical activities with which I often occupied myself during my working hours. (I was working, Jim, just not always on the stuff you were paying me for.)

My most heartfelt thanks to Lorella Loftus for reading the first version of this book and making many suggestions that were incorporated in its eventual revision, and to the good people at Allworth Press, especially Tad Crawford, Monica Rodriguez, Michael Madole, Derek Bacchus, Timothy Cooper and most especially my editor, Nicole Potter. I'm not sure words can adequately express my gratitude to you, Nicole.

Lastly, I'd like to thank the actors—*all* of you, the easy to work with, the difficult, and everyone in between—who worked with me as a fellow and who allowed me to direct them in plays, and to ask their forgiveness. I didn't always do the right thing for the right reason—but I think I'm okay now.

Thank you, all of you, for helping me be who I am.

Love,

Barry

Index

St. Louis Community College
at Meramec
LIBRARY

About the Author

Barry Pineo, a native of Maine and, since 1986, a resident of Texas, recently celebrated his thirtieth year of participating in live theater. While he has written a few plays (notably *Burnt, In Chains,* and *Killers*) and directed and acted in more than he can recall, his greatest passion is for helping people discover their endless potential for storytelling. He has had the privilege of doing exactly that since 2001 as the leader and one of the founding members of the Austin Acting Workshop. For many years he also has written previews and reviews for the Austin *Chronicle* and believes he's learned at least as much from watching as from doing. He presently lives in Round Rock, Texas, and hopes that, if you should ever require a challenging yet nurturing guide to the technique outlined herein, you will consider him for short-term teaching appointments, seminars, workshops, and the like. He can be contacted by writing to bpineo@austin.rr.com.

Books from Allworth Press

Allworth Press is an imprint of Allworth Communications, Inc. Selected titles are listed below.

Improv for Actors
by Dan Diggles (paperback, 6 × 9, 224 pages, $19.95)

Mastering Shakespeare: An Acting Class in Seven Scenes
by Scott Kaiser (paperback, 6 × 9, 256 pages, $19.95)

Movement for Actors
edited by Nicole Potter (paperback, 6 × 9, 288 pages, $19.95)

Promoting Your Acting Career: A Step-by-Step Guide to Opening the Right Doors, Second Edition
by Glenn Alterman (paperback, 6 × 9, 240 pages, $19.95)

An Actor's Guide—Making It in New York City
by Glenn Alterman (paperback, 6 × 9, 288 pages, $19.95)

Creating Your Own Monologue
by Glenn Alterman (paperback, 6 × 9, 208 pages, $14.95)

Making It on Broadway: Actor's Tales of Climbing to the Top
by David Wiener and Jodie Langel (paperback, 6 × 9, 288 pages, $19.95)

Producing Your Own Showcase
by Paul Harris (paperback, 6 × 9, 240 pages, $18.95)

The Perfect Stage Crew: The Compleat Technical Guide for High School, College, and Community Theater
by John Kaluta (paperback, 6 × 9, 256 pages, $19.95)

Please write to request our free catalog. To order by credit card, call 1-800-491-2808 or send a check or money order to Allworth Press, 10 East 23rd Street, Suite 510, New York, NY 10010. Include $5 for shipping and handling for the first book ordered and $1 for each additional book. Ten dollars plus $1 for each additional book if ordering from Canada. New York State residents must add sales tax.

To see our complete catalog on the World Wide Web, or to order online, you can find us at
www.allworth.com.